The
WORST-CASE SCENARIO
2003 Survival Calendar

A WEEK-BY-WEEK GUIDE
TO SURVIVING A YEAR'S WORTH OF PERIL

By Joshua Piven and David Borgenicht

CHRONICLE BOOKS

ACKNOWLEDGMENTS: Many thanks to all of the experts who contributed their knowledge and experience to this calendar, as well as to Erin Slonaker, Jennifer Shenk, Alison Rooney, and Stephanie O'Neill for their creative research and thinking, to Kerry Tessaro for her thoughtful editing, to Craig Hetzer for his creative vision, to Jay Schaefer for helping to start it all, and to the entire team at Chronicle Books.

Designed by Kirk Roberts
Illustrations by Brenda Brown

A Quirk Book
www.quirkproductions.com

ISBN 0-8118-3448-4

Manufactured in China

Distributed in Canada by
Raincoast Books
9050 Shaughnessy Street
Vancouver, B.C. V6P 6E5

Chronicle Books LLC
85 Second Street
San Francisco, CA 94105
www.chroniclebooks.com

Visit www.worstcasescenarios.com
for additional information, updates, and more.

Introduction

When you get to the end of your rope, tie a knot and hang on.
—Franklin Delano Roosevelt

It is our sincere hope that this little calendar will give you the tools, the knowledge, and the skills you need to tie that knot. And to make sure it stays tied.

Welcome to the 2003 edition of *The Worst-Case Scenario Survival Calendar*—very likely the only calendar to make the claim that it could save your life. Sure, it's unlikely that you'll encounter most of the situations within these pages. The odds are much greater that you'll slip on a bar of soap getting out of the shower than that you'll ever encounter a tsunami, an avalanche, a piranha, or quicksand.

But, we've said it before, and we'll say it again: You just never know. And we want you to be prepared for whatever the new year holds in store.

According to *The U.S. Army Survival Manual*, the principles of survival can be conveniently found within the word itself:

Size up the situation
Undue haste makes waste
Remember where you are
Vanquish fear and panic
Improvise
Value living
Act like a native
Live by your wits, but Learn basic skills

Once again, we've worked with our team of experts to come up with clear, step-by-step instructions for surviving life's sudden turns for the worse—those basic skills you'll need to make it out alive from virtually any life- or limb-threatening situation. Culled from the pages of our best-selling titles, *The Worst-Case Scenario Survival Handbook*, *The Worst-Case Scenario Survival Handbook: Travel*, and *The Worst-Case Scenario Survival Handbook: Dating & Sex* (containing perhaps the most treacherous situations of all), and with dozens of extra survival tidbits thrown in, the information in this year's calendar comes from FBI agents, detectives, stuntmen, survival trainers, safari operators, demolition derby drivers, and many more experts in the situations at hand. When you're done reading, you'll very likely be an expert yourself (see letter "A" above).

And once again, we've peppered the calendar with facts, trivia, and essential survival tips to inform, entertain, and sometimes amuse. You'll learn about disastrous dates in history, which months might pose the most serious threats, and a few humorous pieces of information to know and share. After all, maintaining a positive outlook is key (see "V"—everyone knows that laughter can help you "vanquish" your fear).

From How to Perform a Tracheotomy to How to Climb out of a Well, from How to Escape a Bad Date to How to Escape from a Sinking Car, we hope this calendar gives you the tools you need to survive the upcoming year. At the very least, it should certainly help to keep you on track and organized (see "R" above). And maybe, just maybe, it will save your life.

Well, in a pinch, it can always be used for kindling.

—The Authors

HOW TO JUMP
FROM A MOVING CAR

1 Pull the emergency brake.
This may not stop the car, but it might slow it down enough to make jumping safer.

2 Open the car door.

3 Make sure you jump at an angle that will take you out of the path of the car.

4 Tuck in your head and your arms and legs.

5 Aim for a soft landing site: grass, brush, wood chips, anything but pavement or a tree.

6 Roll when you hit the ground.

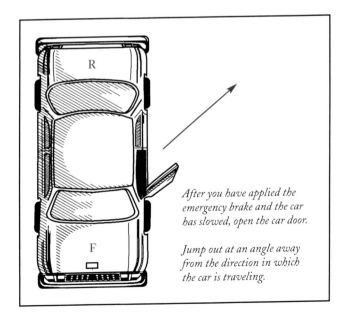

R

F

After you have applied the emergency brake and the car has slowed, open the car door.

Jump out at an angle away from the direction in which the car is traveling.

DECEMBER/JANUARY

Monday **30**	Tuesday **31**	Wednesday **1**
		New Year's Day

Thursday **2** *New Moon* ●	Friday **3**	Saturday **4**
		1958—Sir Edmund Hillary reaches the South Pole over land.

		Sunday **5**
	1841—Herman Melville ships out on the whaler *Acushnet*.	1779—Zebulon Montgomery Pike, explorer, is born.
	1899—A *New York Times* editorial refers to an "automobile"—the first known use of the word.	1825—Alexandre Dumas père fights his first duel.

★ **Tip of the Week:**

Do not attempt to jump from a moving car unless you have absolutely no alternative (say, your car is about to roll off a cliff and the brakes have gone out). In the movies and on television, experienced stuntpeople execute these jumps, and trick photography makes it seem as if the cars are moving much faster than they really are.

December

S	M	T	W	T	F	S
1	2	3	4	5	6	7
8	9	10	11	12	13	14
15	16	17	18	19	20	21
22	23	24	25	26	27	28
29	30	31				

January

S	M	T	W	T	F	S
				1	2	3	4
5	6	7	8	9	10	11
12	13	14	15	16	17	18
19	20	21	22	23	24	25
26	27	28	29	30	31	

HOW TO SURVIVE
A HOSTAGE SITUATION

1 Stay calm.
Help others around you to do the same—remember that the hijackers or hostage takers are extremely nervous and scared. Do not make them more so.

2 If shots are fired, keep your head down and drop to the floor.
If you can, get behind something, but do not move far—your captors may think that you are attempting an escape or an attack.

3 Carefully follow your captors' directions.
Remain alert, and do not try to escape or be a hero. If you are told to put your hands over your head, to keep your head down, or to get into another body position, do it. It may be uncomfortable, but do not change positions. Talk yourself into relaxing into the position—you may need to stay that way for some time. Prepare yourself mentally and emotionally for a long ordeal.

4 Keep the following tips in mind throughout the ordeal:
• Do not make any sudden movements.
• Do not attempt to hide your wallet, passport, ticket, or belongings.
• If your captors speak to you, respond in a regulated tone of voice.
• Carefully observe the characteristics and behavior of the hijackers. Give them nicknames in your mind so that you can identify them. Be prepared to describe them—attire, accents, facial characteristics, height, any aspect that might later help authorities.

5 If you or another hostage is in need of assistance (due to illness or discomfort), solicit a crew member or group leader first.

6 If you are singled out by the captors, be responsive but do not volunteer information.

7 If a rescue attempt is made, remain calm and get down on the ground.
Rescue attempts often involve gunfire.

JANUARY

Monday
6

1412—Joan of Arc is born.

1839—"The Big Wind," a storm of gale-
and, later, hurricane-force wind, begins
off the Irish coast.

Tuesday
7

1904—CQD ("Come Quick Danger") radio
distress signal is adopted. Predates SOS.

Wednesday
8

1800—The feral child known as the
Wild Boy of Aveyron is discovered in
southern France.

Thursday
9

1935—Bob Denver, from TV's
Gilligan's Island, is born.

Friday
First Quarter ☾
10

Saturday
11

Sunday
12

1876—Jack London, author of
The Call of the Wild, is born.

1944—Alfred Hitchcock's *Lifeboat*
opens in theaters.

★ **Tips of the Week:**

- The characteristics of a rescue attempt will be similar to the hijackers'
  takeover—noise, chaos, possibly shooting.
- Expect to be treated as a hijacker or co-conspirator by the rescue force;
  initially you will be treated roughly until the rescuers determine that
  you are not part of the hijacking team.

January

S	M	T	W	T	F	S
			1	2	3	4
5	6	7	8	9	10	11
12	13	14	15	16	17	18
19	20	21	22	23	24	25
26	27	28	29	30	31	

HOW TO SURVIVE A FLASH FLOOD

1 If inside, check the water level outside.
If it is deeper than one foot, do not attempt to drive away. Cars can be swept away in as little as two feet of water.

2 If the water inside is not rising quickly or flowing fast, turn off the power to the building and stay indoors.
Only enter a bàsement if the water is not rising fast. Turn off gas at the main valve to the building. If the water is knee deep, never enter the basement—you may become trapped and drown.

3 If the water level outside is deeper than three feet or seems to be rising or flowing quickly, evacuate the building.

4 Find a flotation device for each person leaving the building.
These can be personal flotation devices (lifejackets) or, if unavailable, couch or chair cushions. Plastic, sealable bags filled with air and placed under a tucked shirt can also provide flotation.

5 Leave the building and move to higher ground.
Do not attempt to drive a car in standing water more than half a foot deep. Proceed to higher ground on foot or in a boat, depending on the depth of water.

JANUARY

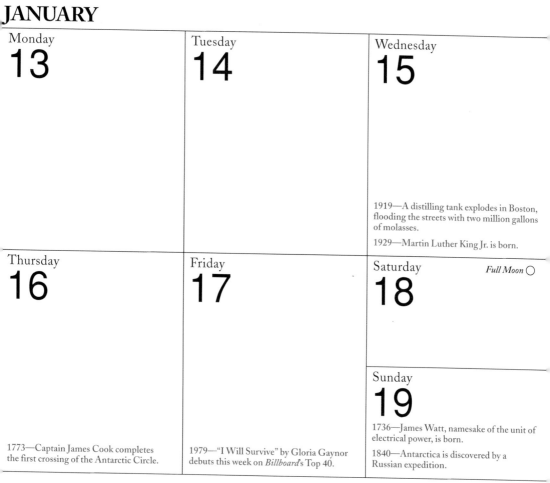

Monday
13

Tuesday
14

Wednesday
15

1919—A distilling tank explodes in Boston, flooding the streets with two million gallons of molasses.

1929—Martin Luther King Jr. is born.

Thursday
16

Friday
17

Saturday   *Full Moon* ○
18

Sunday
19

1736—James Watt, namesake of the unit of electrical power, is born.

1840—Antarctica is discovered by a Russian expedition.

1773—Captain James Cook completes the first crossing of the Antarctic Circle.

1979—"I Will Survive" by Gloria Gaynor debuts this week on *Billboard*'s Top 40.

★ **Tip of the Week:**

After the flood, wear boots and waders when reentering buildings. Do not eat any food that was in the flood, including canned goods; flood waters carry chemicals and disease. Pump out flooded basements gradually (about one-third of the water per day) to avoid structural damage.

January

S	M	T	W	T	F	S
				1	2	3	4
5	6	7	8	9	10	11
12	13	14	15	16	17	18
19	20	21	22	23	24	25
26	27	28	29	30	31	

HOW TO SURVIVE ADRIFT AT SEA

1 Stay aboard your boat as long as possible before you get into a life raft.
In a maritime emergency, the rule of thumb is that you should step up into your raft, meaning you should be up to your waist in water before you get into the raft. Your best chance of survival is on a boat, even a disabled one, not in a life raft.

2 Get in the life raft, and take whatever supplies you can.
Most importantly, if you have water in jugs, take it with you. If you must, throw the jugs of water overboard and tie them to the raft so that you can get them later—they will float. Many canned foods, particularly vegetables, are packed in water, so take them with you if you can.

3 Protect yourself from the elements.
If you are in a cold water/weather environment, get warm. If you can provide yourself with some cover from the sun, do so. You are more likely to die of exposure or hypothermia than of anything else.

4 Put on dry clothes if possible and stay out of the water.
Prolonged exposure to saltwater can damage your skin and cause lesions, which are prone to infection.

5 Find food, if you can.
Life rafts include fishing hooks in their survival kits. If your raft is floating for several weeks, seaweed will form on its underside and fish will naturally congregate in the shade under you. You can catch them with the hook and eat the flesh raw. If no hook is available, you can fashion one using wire or even shards of aluminum from an empty can.

6 Try to get to land, if you know where it is.
Most rafts include small paddles. However, life rafts are not very maneuverable, especially in any wind above three knots. Do not exhaust yourself.

JANUARY

Monday ## 20	Tuesday ## 21	Wednesday ## 22
	1935—The Wilderness Society forms. 1954—The first atomic submarine, the USS *Nautilus*, is launched.	
Martin Luther King Jr. Day		

Thursday ## 23	Friday ## 24	Saturday *Last Quarter* ☽ ## 25
		Sunday ## 26
1909—The first radio rescue at sea is made. 1950—Richard Dean Anderson, from TV's *MacGyver*, is born.	1915—Ernest Borgnine, from *The Poseidon Adventure*, is born.	1915—Rocky Mountain National Park is established.

★ **Tip of the Week:**

Do not ration water: Drink it as needed, but do not drink more than is necessary—a half-gallon a day should be sufficient if you limit your activity.

January

S	M	T	W	T	F	S
			1	2	3	4
5	6	7	8	9	10	11
12	13	14	15	16	17	18
19	20	21	22	23	24	25
26	27	28	29	30	31	

ALEXANDER SELKIRK

In September 1704, a hot-tempered young English sailor demanded to be let off his ship, the result of a quarrel with his captain, William Dampier. The captain willingly obliged, and Alexander Selkirk was marooned on a deserted island in the middle of the Pacific Ocean.

He took a few supplies: his clothes and bedding, a knife, a kettle, a hatchet, his musket and some powder, and a Bible. The first few months alone were terrifying, and he rarely ventured away from the beach. But when sea lions invaded the shores, he fled inland, discovering a lushly vegetated oasis.

Selkirk searched the horizon daily for sign of a ship that could save him from his isolation. Luckily, the island offered him everything he could need, with many edible plants, wild goats, and even wild cats for company. Eventually, he domesticated a few goats and was able to have milk.

For four and a half years, Selkirk lived alone on the island, through rough winters and hot summers. Finally, in February of 1709, he spotted a British ship off shore. He lit fires and was able to draw the attention of the captain aboard, Woodes Rogers, who sent out a search party to investigate. They took Selkirk on, appointed him Mate, and he picked up right where he had left off, sailing with Rogers for two years before returning home.

A true survivor, Selkirk would become the inspiration for Daniel DeFoe's *Robinson Crusoe*, and in the pages of that book his story lives on.

JANUARY/FEBRUARY

Monday **27**	Tuesday **28**	Wednesday **29**
1888—The National Geographic Society is founded in Washington, D.C.	1815—U.S. Coast Guard is created. Their motto: *Semper Paratus* (Always Ready).	

Thursday **30**	Friday **31**	Saturday **1** *New Moon* ●
		National Heart Month begins. National Canned Food Month begins.
1790—The first lifeboat is tested.		**Sunday 2** Groundhog Day 1709—British sailor Alexander Selkirk is rescued after being marooned on a deserted island for five years.

★ **Tip of the Week:**

To find water on a deserted island, tie rags or tufts of fine grass to your ankles and walk in grass or foliage at sunrise. The dew will gather on the material, which can be wrung out into a container.

January

S	M	T	W	T	F	S
				1	2	3	4
5	6	7	8	9	10	11
12	13	14	15	16	17	18
19	20	21	22	23	24	25
26	27	28	29	30	31	

February

S	M	T	W	T	F	S
						1
2	3	4	5	6	7	8
9	10	11	12	13	14	15
16	17	18	19	20	21	22
23	24	25	26	27	28	

HOW TO ESCAPE
FROM A MOUNTAIN LION

1 Do not run.
The animal will most likely have both seen and smelled you already, and mountain lions can easily outrun humans.

2 Try to make yourself appear bigger.
Do not crouch down; a mountain lion is less likely to attack a larger animal. Open your coat wide or pick up small children who are with you. Hold your ground, wave your hands, and shout. Show the mountain lion that you are not defenseless.

3 Back away slowly or wait until the animal moves away.
Report any lion sightings to authorities as soon as possible.

Upon sighting a mountain lion, do not run. Do not crouch down. Try to make yourself appear larger by opening wide your coat.

4 If the lion behaves aggressively or attacks, throw stones and fight back.
Convince the lion that you are dangerous yourself. Most mountain lions are small enough that an average-size human will be able to fight it off successfully. Hit the mountain lion in the head, especially around the eyes and mouth. Use sticks, fists, or whatever is at hand. Do not curl up and play dead.

FEBRUARY

Monday
3

1973—President Nixon signs the
Endangered Species Act into law.

Tuesday
4

Wednesday
5

1936—The National Wildlife
Federation forms.

Thursday
6

Friday
7

1989—Sardines rain on the town of Ipswich,
Australia. Scientists suspect a storm caused
updrafts that carried the fish into the atmos-
phere.

Saturday
8

1910—Boy Scouts of America is founded.
Their motto: Be prepared.

Sunday
9

First Quarter ☾

★ Tip of the Week:

If you are attacked by a mountain lion, protect your neck and throat at all
costs. Mountain lions generally leap down upon prey from above and deliver a
"killing bite" to the back of the neck. Their technique is to break the neck and
knock down the prey, and they also will rush and lunge up at the neck, dragging
the victim down while holding the neck in a crushing grip.

February

S	M	T	W	T	F	S
						1
2	3	4	5	6	7	8
9	10	11	12	13	14	15
16	17	18	19	20	21	22
23	24	25	26	27	28	

HOW TO FIND DIRECTION WITHOUT A COMPASS

STAR METHOD

Northern Hemisphere
Locate the North Star, Polaris.
The North Star is the last star in the handle of the Little Dipper. Walking toward it means you are walking north. You can use the Big Dipper to find the North Star. A straight, imaginary line drawn between the two stars at the end of the Big Dipper's bowl will point to the North Star. The distance to the North Star is about five times the distance between the two "pointer" stars.

Southern Hemisphere
Find the Southern Cross.
The Southern Cross is a group of four bright stars in the shape of a cross and tilted to one side. Imagine the long axis extends in a line five times its actual length. The point where this line ends is south. If you can view the horizon, draw an imaginary line straight down to create a southern landmark.

MOSS METHOD

Locate moss.
Mosses grow in places with lots of shade and water: areas that are cool and moist. On tree trunks, the north sides tend to be more shady and moist than the south sides; therefore, moss usually grows on the north sides of trees. However, this method is not infallible—in many forests, both sides of a tree can be shady and moist.

FEBRUARY

Monday
10

1774—Andrew Becker demonstrates his diving suit in the Thames.

Tuesday
11

1752—Pennsylvania Hospital, the first hospital in the U.S., officially opens in Philadelphia.

1847—Thomas Alva Edison is born.

Wednesday
12

1809—Abraham Lincoln is born.

Thursday
13

Friday
14

Valentine's Day

Saturday
15

1564—Galileo Galilei is born.

1874—Ernest Shackleton, captain of the *Endurance*, is born.

Sunday
16

Full Moon ○

★ **Tip of the Week:**

You can also get a sense of direction by paying attention to the movement of clouds: Generally, weather moves from east to west.

February

S	M	T	W	T	F	S
						1
2	3	4	5	6	7	8
9	10	11	12	13	14	15
16	17	18	19	20	21	22
23	24	25	26	27	28	

HOW TO SURVIVE IN A PLUMMETING ELEVATOR

Elevators have numerous safety features. There have been very few recorded incidents involving death from plummeting elevators. In general, it is highly unlikely for a cable (also called traction) elevator to fall all the way to the bottom of the shaft. Moreover, the compressed air column in the elevator hoistway and the car buffers at the bottom of the hoistway may keep the forces of the impact survivable.

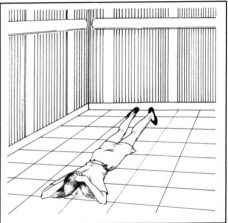

1 Flatten your body against the car floor.
While there is disagreement among the experts, most recommend this method. This should distribute the force of impact, rather than concentrate it on one area of your body. (Standing may be difficult anyway.)

2 Cover your face and head to protect them from ceiling parts that may break loose.

FEBRUARY

Monday
17

Presidents' Day

Tuesday
18

Wednesday
19

Thursday
20

1872—Cyrus Baldwin patents the hydraulic electric elevator.

Friday
21

1858—The first electric burglar alarm is installed.

1967—Ford Motor Company recalls 217,000 cars to check brakes and steering.

Saturday
22

1732—George Washington is born.

1989—Lightning Strike and Electric Shock Survivors International, Inc. (LSESSI) is founded.

Sunday
23
Last Quarter ☽

★ **Tips of the Week:**
- Hydraulic elevators are more likely than cable elevators to fall. Their height is limited to about 70 feet, so a free fall would probably result in injury—but not death.
- Do not jump just before the elevator hits the bottom. The chances that you will jump at exactly the right time are very small. The elevator may collapse around you and crush you if you are still upright in the car.

February

S	M	T	W	T	F	S
						1
2	3	4	5	6	7	8
9	10	11	12	13	14	15
16	17	18	19	20	21	22
23	24	25	26	27	28	

HOW TO STOP A CAR WITH FAILED BRAKES

1 Begin pumping the brake pedal and keep pumping it.
You may be able to build up enough pressure in the braking system to slow down a bit, or even stop completely. Even if you have anti-lock brakes, this method may work.

2 Shift the car into the lowest gear possible and let the engine and transmission slow you down.
If you have room, swerve the car back and forth across the road to decrease your speed even more.

3 Gently pull up the emergency brake (also called the hand brake or parking brake).
Pulling too hard will cause the rear wheels to lock, spinning the car around. In most cars, the emergency brake is cable operated and serves as a fail-safe brake that should work even when the rest of the braking system has failed.

4 Look for something to help stop you.
A flat or uphill road that intersects with the road you are on, a field, or a fence will slow you further but not stop you suddenly. Avoid trees and wooden telephone poles; they do not yield easily. Do not attempt to sideswipe oncoming cars.

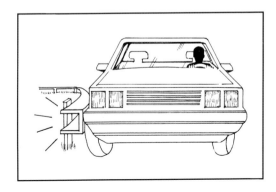

FEBRUARY/MARCH

Monday
24

Tuesday
25

Wednesday
26

1919—Congress establishes Grand Canyon National Park.

Thursday
27

Friday
28

Saturday
1

1872—Yellowstone, the nation's first national park, is established.

Sunday   *New Moon* ●
2

1902—John Steinbeck, author of *The Grapes of Wrath*, is born.

1934—Consumer advocate Ralph Nader, author of *Unsafe at Any Speed*, is born.

1949—Captain James Gallagher and his crew complete the first nonstop around-the-world flight.

★ **Tip of the Week:**

If you are coming up behind another car and cannot stop, try to use the other car as a braking measure. Hit the car square, bumper to bumper, so you do not knock the other car off the road. This maneuver works best if the vehicle in front of you is larger than your own and if both vehicles are traveling at similar speeds.

February

S	M	T	W	T	F	S
						1
2	3	4	5	6	7	8
9	10	11	12	13	14	15
16	17	18	19	20	21	22
23	24	25	26	27	28	

March

S	M	T	W	T	F	S
						1
2	3	4	5	6	7	8
9	10	11	12	13	14	15
16	17	18	19	20	21	22
23/30	24/31	25	26	27	28	29

HOW TO TREAT
A SCORPION STING

Most species of scorpion have venom of low to moderate toxicity and do not pose a serious health threat to adult humans, other than severe pain.

1 Apply heat or cold packs to the sting site for pain relief.
The most severe pain usually occurs at the site of the sting. Also use an analgesic (painkiller) if available.

2 If an allergic reaction occurs, take an antihistamine.
Scorpion venom contains histamines, which may cause allergic reactions (asthma, rashes) in sensitive persons.

3 Watch for an irregular heartbeat, tingling in extremities, an inability to move limbs or fingers, or difficulty breathing.
Most scorpion stings cause instantaneous pain at the site of the sting. The pain may radiate over the body several minutes after the initial sting. Pain tends to be felt in joints, especially in the armpits and groin. Systemic symptoms may also occur—possibly numbness in the face, mouth, or throat; muscle twitches; sweating; nausea; vomiting; fever; and restlessness. These symptoms are normal and not life-threatening, and usually subside in one to three hours. The site of the sting may remain sore for one to three days.

4 Seek emergency medical care if you exhibit the above symptoms. An adult will survive even if it takes 12 hours or more to get to a hospital, but a small child will need medical care immediately.

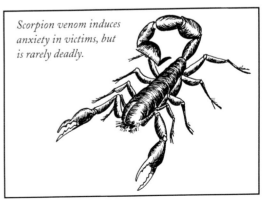

Scorpion venom induces anxiety in victims, but is rarely deadly.

5 Do not apply tourniquets.
The toxins are small and move extremely rapidly away from the site of the sting.

MARCH

Monday **3**	Tuesday **4**	Wednesday **5**
1513—Ponce de Leon begins his quest for the Fountain of Youth.		Ash Wednesday

Thursday **6**	Friday **7**	Saturday **8**
		Sunday **9**
1836—Siege at the Alamo ends. No one survives. 1899—"Aspirin" is registered as a trademark by the Bayer company in Germany.		National Panic Day 1454—Amerigo Vespucci is born.

★ **Tip of the Week:**

If you have been stung by a scorpion, never cut the wound or allow anyone to suck out the poison. This can cause infection or transfer the venom into the bloodstream of the person attempting to remove the poison.

March

S	M	T	W	T	F	S
						1
2	3	4	5	6	7	8
9	10	11	12	13	14	15
16	17	18	19	20	21	22
23/30	24/31	25	26	27	28	29

HOW TO SURVIVE AN AVALANCHE

1 Stay on top of the snow by using a freestyle swimming motion.

2 If you are buried, determine which way is up.
If you still have a ski pole with you, poke through the snow in several directions until you see or feel open air. If you do not have a ski pole, create a space around your face and spit in it. The saliva should head straight down.

3 Dig yourself out.
If you are not too injured, attempt to dig your way toward the open air. Scoop the snow out of the way using your hands or kick the snow with your feet.

Struggle to stay on top of the snow by using a freestyle swimming motion.

MARCH

Monday *First Quarter* ☾	Tuesday	Wednesday
# 10	# 11	# 12
1980—Prince Charles narrowly escapes an avalanche at a Swiss ski resort.	1888—The "Great Blizzard of '88" begins to roar along the Atlantic seaboard.	1912—Girl Scouts of America is founded.

Thursday	Friday	Saturday
# 13	# 14	# 15
		Ides of March
		Sunday
		# 16
1887—Earmuffs are patented by Chester Greenwood.	1879—Albert Einstein is born.	

★**Tips of the Week:**

- Never go hiking or skiing alone in avalanche territory.
- Be aware that avalanches occur in areas with new snow; in the afternoons of sunny days (when the morning sun may have loosened the snowpack); and on mountainsides with angles of thirty to forty-five degrees.
- Always carry a beacon. The beacon broadcasts your position by creating a magnetic field that can be picked up by other members of your group.

March

S	M	T	W	T	F	S
						1
2	3	4	5	6	7	8
9	10	11	12	13	14	15
16	17	18	19	20	21	22
23/30	24/31	25	26	27	28	29

HOW TO SURVIVE WHEN LOST IN THE JUNGLE

1 Find civilization.
Most civilizations are formed along rivers, and the water is the fastest way for you to travel. To find a river, follow animal trails; they generally lead toward water.

2 Fashion a makeshift raft.
Use whatever is handy—tarps, brush, and saplings can be lashed together to create a raft.

3 Let the current carry you downstream.

4 Travel on the rivers only during daylight hours.
Alligators and crocodiles are night hunters, so avoid traveling on water at night.

5 Watch closely for signs of villages or settlements.

MARCH

Monday **17**	Tuesday **18** *Full Moon* ○	Wednesday **19**
St. Patrick's Day 1910—Camp Fire Girls organization is founded.	1931—The electric razor is manufactured for the first time.	1821—English explorer Sir Richard Burton is born.

Thursday **20**	Friday **21**	Saturday **22**
		1630—The New York Horticultural Society is incorporated.

Sunday **23**

	Friday column	
Equinox	1871—British journalist Henry Stanley begins his expedition to Africa to find Scottish explorer Dr. David Livingstone— together they seek the source of the Nile.	

★ **Tip of the Week:**

If you must travel on land, mark your trail by breaking and turning over fresh vegetation. This will reveal the bright undersides of leaves and will leave a clear trail should you need to backtrack.

March

S	M	T	W	T	F	S
						1
2	3	4	5	6	7	8
9	10	11	12	13	14	15
16	17	18	19	20	21	22
23/30	24/31	25	26	27	28	29

HOW TO DEAL
WITH A STALKER

1 Firmly inform the stalker that if the unwanted behavior persists, you will take action.
Threaten to contact authorities or a larger, stronger friend or relative. Be prepared to do so. Do not give in to any threats, and be ready to secure a restraining order or civil protection order if it becomes necessary for your peace of mind.

2 Inform your family, friends, and coworkers of the situation.

3 Keep a paper trail.
Save any relevant letters, notes, e-mails, and voicemails—anything that can provide evidence of unwanted attention. Maintain a log or diary of your stalker's actions and report any unlawful behavior to the police immediately. Report phone calls to both the phone company and the police.

4 Inform authorities.
Do not let fear of retribution stop you from taking action. Take legal action immediately.

MARCH

Monday
Last Quarter ☾
24

1874—Erich Weiss, aka Harry Houdini, is born.

Tuesday
25

1997—Former president George Bush, 72 years old, parachutes from a plane over the Arizona desert.

Wednesday
26

1845—The lifeboat is patented by Joseph Francis.

Thursday
27

1513—Ponce de Leon "discovers" Florida.

Friday
28

1866—The first hospital ambulance goes into service.

Saturday
29

Sunday
30

1981—John W. Hinckley Jr. shoots President Ronald Reagan in an attempt to win Jodie Foster's favor.

★ **Tip of the Week:**

If you move to a new house at any point during the stalking, make sure that your new address is unlisted. Contact the department of motor vehicles and the voter registration bureau to have them block your address. Forward your mail to a P.O. Box, and do not accept any packages unless you are certain of where they came from.

March

S	M	T	W	T	F	S
						1
2	3	4	5	6	7	8
9	10	11	12	13	14	15
16	17	18	19	20	21	22
23/30	24/31	25	26	27	28	29

HOW TO FOOL
A LIE DETECTOR TEST

1 During the pre-test, force yourself to breathe faster than normal.
Examiners will administer a pre-test before the actual polygraph to create a
baseline of reactions. Breathing faster will skew the results to make you appear
"normal" when nervous.

2 During the pre-test, display confidence. Never appear nervous or shy.

3 Maintain eye contact with the examiner. Do not fidget.
Do not, however, sit completely still. Move something subtly but regularly: your
toes, fingers, hips, etc.

4 Do not try to anticipate the questions you will be asked. Think positive and
relaxing thoughts.

5 When answering control questions truthfully, bite your tongue slightly.
This will hopefully give a false reading—they may find that it is impossible to
decipher your test because the readings are inconsistent (answers show stress
both when you're answering truthfully and when you could be lying).

MARCH/APRIL

Monday	Tuesday	Wednesday
31	**1** *New Moon* ●	**2**
	April Fools' Day 1964—The first travel accident policy is issued.	1978—Velcro debuts on the market.

Thursday	Friday	Saturday
3	**4**	**5**
		1971—Fran Phipps becomes the first woman to reach the North Pole.

Sunday

6

1909—Admiral Robert Peary becomes the first man to reach the North Pole.

★ **Tip of the Week:**

Remember that a lie detector test is subject to interpretation, and a test is only as good as the examiner. If the examiner deems the results inconclusive, you will likely not be required to pass another lie detector test.

March

S	M	T	W	T	F	S
						1
2	3	4	5	6	7	8
9	10	11	12	13	14	15
16	17	18	19	20	21	22
23/30	24/31	25	26	27	28	29

April

S	M	T	W	T	F	S
		1	2	3	4	5
6	7	8	9	10	11	12
13	14	15	16	17	18	19
20	21	22	23	24	25	26
27	28	29	30			

HOW TO GET TO THE SURFACE IF YOUR SCUBA TANK RUNS OUT OF AIR

1 Signal to your fellow divers that you are having a problem: point to your tank or regulator.

2 If someone comes to your aid, share the regulator, passing it back and forth while swimming slowly to the surface.
Take two breaths, then pass it back to the other diver. Ascend together, exhaling as you do. Then take another two breaths, alternating, until you reach the surface. Nearly all divers carry an extra regulator connected to their tank.

3 If no one can help you, keep your regulator in your mouth.
Air may expand in the tank as you ascend, allowing you to take additional breaths.

4 Look directly up so that your airway is as straight as possible.

5 Swim to the surface at a slow to moderate rate, exhaling continuously as you swim up.
It is very important that you exhale the entire way up, but the rate that you exhale is also important. Exhale slowly: do not exhaust all your air in the first few seconds of your ascent. As long as you are even slightly exhaling, your passageway will be open and air can vent from your lungs.

Keep your regulator in your mouth.

Keep your airway as straight as possible by looking toward the surface.

Swim at a slow to moderate rate, exhaling continuously.

APRIL

Monday
7

1954—Jackie Chan is born.

Tuesday
8

Wednesday
9
First Quarter ☾

1865—Lee surrenders to Grant, ending the U.S. Civil War.

1872—Dried milk is patented.

Thursday
10

1849—The safety pin is patented.

Friday
11

1900—The U.S. Navy acquires its first submarine.

Saturday
12

Sunday
13

Palm Sunday

1962—Rachel Carson's book *Silent Spring* is published.

★ **Tips of the Week:**

• Controlled Emergency Swimming Ascent (CESA) should not be performed from any depth greater than 130 feet.

• If you do not exhale continuously, you risk an aneurysm.

April

S	M	T	W	T	F	S
		1	2	3	4	5
6	7	8	9	10	11	12
13	14	15	16	17	18	19
20	21	22	23	24	25	26
27	28	29	30			

HOW TO MAKE
A DEADFALL ANIMAL TRAP

1 Find three straight sticks that are roughly the same length and diameter, and a large, heavy stone.
The length and thickness of the sticks you need will depend on the weight of the stone—the heavier the stone, the larger the sticks need to be.

2 Cut a square notch at the center of one stick and cut one end to a point like that of a flathead screwdriver.
This is your upright support bar.

3 Cut a square notch (to fit into the first squared notch like a Lincoln Log) in the middle of the second stick.
At one end of this stick, cut a triangular notch a few inches from the end. Whittle the opposite end to a point. This is your bait bar.

4 Cut a triangular notch into the middle of the last stick and cut one end to a point like that of a flathead screwdriver.
This is your locking bar.

5 Assemble the trap.
Anchor the support stick vertically into the ground. Attach a piece of food to the end of the bait bar and match the two square notches together as in the diagram. Place the locking bar atop the support and bait bars, forming a 45-degree angle with the bait bar.

locking bar

upright support bar   bait bar

6 Lean the stone against the locking bar.
When an animal takes the bait, it will dislodge the bait and locking bars, triggering the deadfall. The prey will be trapped or crushed beneath the stone.

APRIL

Monday
14

1912—The *Titanic* sinks—711 people survive.

Tuesday
15

1800—Sir James Clark Ross, discoverer of the magnetic North Pole, is born.

Wednesday
16

Full Moon ○

1867—Wilbur Wright, American aviation pioneer, is born.

Thursday
17

Passover

1629—The first commercial fishery is established.

1629—The first horses are imported to the U.S.

Friday
18

Good Friday

Saturday
19

Sunday
20

Easter

★ **Tips of the Week:**

• To increase the odds of catching an animal, set multiple traps along worn paths.

• Check the traps only once or twice daily.

• Do not build the trap where you intend to place it, or your scent will permeate the area, frightening off animals.

• Be alert when approaching a trapped animal. It may not be dead, and it may attack you.

• Do not leave any traps or trap elements behind when you leave an area.

April

S	M	T	W	T	F	S
		1	2	3	4	5
6	7	8	9	10	11	12
13	14	15	16	17	18	19
20	21	22	23	24	25	26
27	28	29	30			

HOW TO BREAK DOWN A DOOR

INTERIOR DOORS

★ Give the door a well-placed kick or two to the lock area to break it down. Running at the door and slamming against it with your shoulder or body is not usually as effective as kicking with your foot. Your foot exerts more force than your shoulder, and you will be able to direct this force toward the area of the locking mechanism more effectively this way.

EXTERIOR DOORS

★ Give the door several well-placed kicks at the point where the lock is mounted.
An exterior door usually takes several tries to break down this way, so keep at it.

Alternative Method (if you have a sturdy piece of steel):
Wrench or pry the lock off the door by inserting the tool between the lock and the door and prying back and forth.

Exterior doors are of sturdier construction. Kick at the point where the lock is mounted.

APRIL

Monday
21

1982—The first successful heart implant is performed.

Tuesday
22

1970—The first Earth Day is observed in the U.S.

Wednesday
23
Last Quarter ☾

1981—Johnny Cash, Jerry Lee Lewis, and Carl Perkins record the live album *The Survivors*.

Thursday
24

Friday
25

1719—Daniel Defoe's novel *Robinson Crusoe* is published in London.

1939—Federal Security Agency is established.

Saturday
26

1900—Seismologist Charles Richter is born.

Sunday
27

★ **Tip of the Week:**

You can usually determine the construction and solidity of a door by tapping on it. If it sounds hollow or tinny, it will require a moderate amount of force to break down. If it sounds solid, it will require a significantly greater amount of force, or some sort of pry bar.

April

S	M	T	W	T	F	S
		1	2	3	4	5
6	7	8	9	10	11	12
13	14	15	16	17	18	19
20	21	22	23	24	25	26
27	28	29	30			

HOW TO STOP
A RUNAWAY HORSE

1 Hold on tight to the saddle with your hands and thighs.
Most injuries occur when the rider is thrown, falls, or jumps off the horse.

2 Grip the saddle horn or the front of the saddle with one hand and the reins
with the other, sitting up in the saddle as much as you can.
Fight the instinct to lean forward, since this is not the standard position for a
rider when a horse is asked to stop ("Whoa!"), and the horse can feel the difference. Keep a deep seat, with your feet pushed a little forward in the stirrups.

3 Alternately tug and release the reins with a medium pressure.
Never jerk or pull hard on the reins when the horse is running at full speed—you
could pull the horse off-balance and it may stumble or fall. If you have lost hold
of the reins, simply hold onto the saddle horn or the horse's mane until the horse
comes to a stop.

4 When the horse slows down to a slow lope or a trot, pull one rein to the side
with steady pressure so that the horse's head moves to the side, toward your
foot in the stirrup.
This maneuver will cause the horse to walk in a circle. The horse will become
bored, sense that you are in control again, and slow down.

5 When the horse is at a walk, pull back with slow, steady pressure on both reins
until the horse stops completely.

6 Dismount the horse immediately, before it can bolt again.
Hold the reins as you get down to keep the horse from moving.

APRIL/MAY

Monday
28

Tuesday
29

1903—A huge slab of limestone slides off Turtle Mountain in Alberta, Canada, burying a mine entrance. Seventeen trapped miners dig to freedom thirteen hours later.

Wednesday
30

1881—Billy the Kid escapes from the Mesilla, New Mexico jailhouse.

Thursday   *New Moon* ●
1

May Day

Friday
2

Saturday
3

Kentucky Derby

1986—Horse racing legend Bill Shoemaker, 54, rides Ferdinand to victory, becoming the oldest jockey to win the Kentucky Derby.

Sunday
4

1626—Dutch explorer Peter Minuit lands on Manhattan Island.

★ **Tip of the Week:**

Horses bolt when they are frightened or extremely irritated. The key response is to remain in control of the situation without causing the horse greater anxiety. Talk to it reassuringly and rub its neck with one hand. Yelling, screaming, and kicking the horse will only agitate it more.

April

S	M	T	W	T	F	S
		1	2	3	4	5
6	7	8	9	10	11	12
13	14	15	16	17	18	19
20	21	22	23	24	25	26
27	28	29	30			

May

S	M	T	W	T	F	S
					1	2	3
4	5	6	7	8	9	10
11	12	13	14	15	16	17
18	19	20	21	22	23	24
25	26	27	28	29	30	31

HOW TO JUMP
FROM A MOVING TRAIN

1 Make your jump from the end of the last (the rear) car.
If this is not an option, you can jump from the space between cars, or from the door if you can get it open.

2 Wait for the train to slow as it rounds a bend in the tracks, if you have time.

3 Pick your landing spot before you jump.
The ideal spot is relatively soft and free of obstructions. Avoid trees, bushes, and rocks.

4 Get as low to the floor as possible, bending your knees so you can leap away from the train car.

5 Jump perpendicular to the train, leaping as far away from the train as you can.

6 Cover and protect your head with your hands and arms, and roll like a log when you land.
Do NOT roll head over heels as if doing a forward somersault.

Pick your landing spot, and jump as far away from the train as you can. Protect your head.

Try to land so that all parts of your body hit the ground at the same time.

Roll like a log, keeping your head protected.

MAY

Monday	Tuesday	Wednesday
5	**6**	**7**
	1937—The *Hindenburg* zeppelin explodes.	
	1954—Roger Bannister breaks the four-minute mile in Oxford, England.	
1865—The first U.S. train robbery occurs.		1915—The *Lusitania* sinks.

Thursday	Friday *First Quarter* ☾	Saturday
8	**9**	**10**
		1869—A golden spike is driven at Promontory Point, Utah, marking the completion of the first transcontinental railroad in the U.S.

Sunday
11

Mother's Day

1946—Robert Jarvik, inventor of the first artificial heart, is born.

★ **Tip of the Week:**

To soften the blow, stuff blankets, clothing, or seat cushions underneath your clothes, if they are available. Wear a thick jacket if possible. Use a belt to secure some padding around your head, but make certain you can see clearly. Pad your knees, elbows, and hips.

May

S	M	T	W	T	F	S
				1	2	3
4	5	6	7	8	9	10
11	12	13	14	15	16	17
18	19	20	21	22	23	24
25	26	27	28	29	30	31

HOW TO CLIMB
OUT OF A WELL

STEMMING TECHNIQUE

1 Place your right hand and right foot on one wall and your left hand and left foot on the opposite wall.
Your hands should be lower than your shoulders, and your fingers should point down.

2 Keep the pressure on your feet by assuming a somewhat scissored leg stance, with your body facing slightly to the right.

3 Brace yourself by pushing out with your hands.

4 Move one foot quickly up a few inches, followed immediately by moving the other foot up a few inches.

5 Reposition your hands one at a time.

6 Continue until you reach the top, where you will have to grab something sturdy to help you swing up over the edge.

MAY

Monday	Tuesday	Wednesday
12	**13**	**14**
	1999—Rescue workers pull Jesse, a seventeen-month-old baby boy, out of a well in Kansas.	1804—Lewis and Clark expedition begins.

Thursday *Full Moon* ○	Friday	Saturday
15	**16**	**17**
		1875—The first Kentucky Derby is run at Churchill Downs.

Sunday

18

1980—Mt. Saint Helens erupts.

★ **Tip of the Week:**

If you near the opening of the well and there is nothing to grab onto, continue in the same manner until your upper body is out of the well. At this point, flop forward so that the majority of your body is on the ground. Use leverage to climb out.

May

S	M	T	W	T	F	S
				1	2	3
4	5	6	7	8	9	10
11	12	13	14	15	16	17
18	19	20	21	22	23	24
25	26	27	28	29	30	31

HOW TO AVOID AND SURVIVE A HIT AND RUN

1   Always cross streets in a crosswalk and look both ways before crossing.

2   Keep your eyes on both the traffic patterns and the oncoming cars.
Be familiar with the intersection, and know which cars have a green light and which do not. Use the lights to help you cross, but pay more attention to the moving cars—they may not be paying attention to you, or the lights.

3   If a car is headed directly for you, assess the amount of time you have.

4   Dive and roll out of the car's path if you have enough time before impact. You may get some cuts and bruises but you will not get run over.

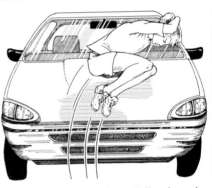

5   If you can't get out of the way, jump as high as you can just before impact. Jump in a tight tuck or ball position, with your arms over your head. Jump in profile with your shoulder toward the car; this exposes fewer vital organs.

6   Brace for impact.
You will probably hit the windshield.

Jump in profile, tucking into a ball and covering your head. Roll onto and off the windshield.

7   Roll onto and off the windshield.

8   Stay rolled into a ball and brace yourself for when you hit the ground. Keep your arms over your head.

9   Try to roll or crawl out of the way of any other cars that might be approaching from both directions.

MAY

Monday **19**	Tuesday **20**	Wednesday **21**
Victoria Day (Canada) 1987—A device to keep a severed head alive is patented by Chet Fleming.		1881—American Red Cross is organized by Clara Barton.

Thursday *Last Quarter* ☽ **22**	Friday **23**	Saturday **24**
		Sunday **25** 1721—The first insurance policy becomes available in the U.S.

★ **Tip of the Week:**

If the vehicle is a large truck (an 18-wheeler) with high clearance and you cannot get out of the way, lie flat, face-down on the ground, feet first, in the same direction as the truck. Try to center yourself between the wheels, and the truck may pass safely over you. Protect your head in case the truck is dragging something beneath it.

May

S	M	T	W	T	F	S
				1	2	3
4	5	6	7	8	9	10
11	12	13	14	15	16	17
18	19	20	21	22	23	24
25	26	27	28	29	30	31

HOW TO ESCAPE FROM A SINKING CAR

1 Open the window as soon as possible. If you have the presence of mind to get the window open before you hit the water, do it. This is your best chance of escape—opening the door will be very difficult due to the outside water pressure. Opening the window allows water to come in and equalize the pressure. Once the water pressure inside and outside the car is equal, you will be able to open the door or even swim out the window.

As soon as you hit the water, open your window. Otherwise, the pressure of the water will make it very difficult to escape.

If you were unable to open the window before hitting the water, attempt to break it with your foot or a heavy object.

2 If your power windows will not work or you cannot roll your windows down all the way, attempt to break the glass. Use your foot or shoulder, a screwdriver, or a heavy object.

3 Get out as soon as you can.
Do not worry about leaving anything behind unless it is another person. Vehicles with the engine in front will sink at a steep angle, and if the water is 15 feet or deeper, the vehicle may end up on its roof, upside down. Depending on the vehicle, floating time will range from a few seconds to a few minutes. The more airtight the car, the longer it floats.

4 If you are unable to open the window or break it, wait until the car fills with water.
Remain calm and do not panic. When the water level reaches your head, take a deep breath and hold it. Now the pressure will be equalized inside and outside, and you should be able to open the door and swim to the surface.

MAY/JUNE

Monday	Tuesday	Wednesday
## 26	## 27	## 28

Memorial Day Observed

1907—John Wayne is born.

1954—Sally Ride, the first woman on a space shuttle, is born.

Thursday	Friday *New Moon* ●	Saturday
## 29	## 30	## 31

1889—The Johnstown Flood, the worst in U.S. history, takes place in southwestern Pennsylvania.

Sunday
1

1953—Sir Edmund Hillary and Sherpa Tenzing Norgay become the first explorers to reach the summit of Mount Everest.

Memorial Day

National Safety Month begins.

1831—The magnetic North Pole is located by James Clark Ross.

★ **Tip of the Week:**

If you are driving your car on a frozen lake, carry several large nails and a length of rope with you. In the event that your car breaks through the ice, the nails will help you pull yourself out of the ice and the rope can be thrown to some-one on more solid ground.

			May			
S	M	T	W	T	F	S
				1	2	3
4	5	6	7	8	9	10
11	12	13	14	15	16	17
18	19	20	21	22	23	24
25	26	27	28	29	30	31

			June			
S	M	T	W	T	F	S
1	2	3	4	5	6	7
8	9	10	11	12	13	14
15	16	17	18	19	20	21
22	23	24	25	26	27	28
29	30					

HOW TO JUMP
FROM ROOF TO ROOF

1 If you have time, look for any obstructions at the ledge.
You may have to clear short walls, gutters, or other obstacles as well as the space between buildings.

2 Check your target building.
Make certain that you have enough space to land and roll. If the target building is lower than your building, assess how much lower it is. You risk broken ankles or legs if there is more than a one story differential in the buildings. Two stories or more and you risk a broken back.

3 Check the distance between the buildings.
Most people cannot jump further than 10 feet, even at a full run. If the buildings are further apart than this distance, you risk catastrophic injury or death. You could successfully leap a span across an alley, but not a two-lane road.

4 Pick a spot for take-off and a spot for landing.

5 Run at full speed toward the edge.
You must be running as fast as you can to attempt a leap of a distance of more than a few feet. You will need 40 to 60 feet to gain enough speed to clear about 10 feet of distance.

6 Leap.
Make sure your center of gravity is over the edge of your target building in case your whole body doesn't clear the span and you have to grab hold. Jump with your arms and hands extended and ready to grab the ledge if necessary.

7 Try to land on your feet, then immediately tuck your head and tumble sideways onto your shoulders, not forward onto your head.

JUNE

Monday
2

1904—Johnny Weismuller, swimming champion and star of *Tarzan*, is born.

Tuesday
3

Wednesday
4

1892—The Sierra Club is incorporated.

Thursday
5

1783—Joseph and Jacques Montgolfier demonstrate their hot-air balloon in a ten-minute flight over Annonay, France.

Friday
6

1936—The first helicopter is tested.

1938—Superman first appears in DC Comics.

Saturday   *First Quarter* ☾
7

Sunday
8

★ **Tip of the Week:**

It is nearly impossible to leap to a building that is more than one story higher than the one you are on. Seek an alternate escape if all the surrounding buildings are taller.

June

S	M	T	W	T	F	S
1	2	3	4	5	6	7
8	9	10	11	12	13	14
15	16	17	18	19	20	21
22	23	24	25	26	27	28
29	30					

HOW TO SAVE SOMEONE WHO IS CHOKING

1 Tell the person to stand up and stay put.
Keep your voice low and firm and your sentences short. Explain that you are going to perform the Heimlich maneuver.

2 Hug the person from behind.
Put your arms around the waist and make a fist with one hand.

3 Place your fist in the solar plexus and the other hand, palm open, over your fist.
The solar plexus is the first soft spot in the center of the body, between the navel and the ribs.

4 Tell the person to bend forward slightly.
If he or she does not respond, push on the upper back.

5 Pull your fist in and up.
Use a quick, forceful motion. This will push out residual lung gas under pressure, clearing any obstructions. Repeat if choking persists.

6 If, after several attempts, choking still persists, instruct the choking victim to bend forward over the back of a chair.
The head of the chair should be at hip-level.

7 Strike between the shoulder blades with the heel of your open hand.
The blow generates gaseous pressure in a blocked airway, and with a head-down position, sometimes works when the Heimlich does not.

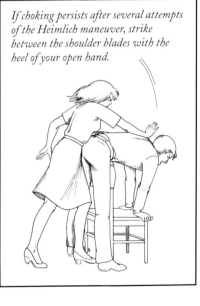

If choking persists after several attempts of the Heimlich maneuver, strike between the shoulder blades with the heel of your open hand.

JUNE

Monday	Tuesday	Wednesday
9	**10**	**11**

1909—The first emergency S.O.S. signal is broadcast via telegraph.

Thursday	Friday	Saturday _Full Moon_ ○
12	**13**	**14**

Flag Day

1974—Dr. Henry Heimlich announces a maneuver to aid choking victims.

Sunday

15

1897—The Swiss Army Knife is legally registered.

1923—Harry Houdini frees himself from a straitjacket while suspended upside down forty feet above the ground in New York City.

Father's Day

1752—Benjamin Franklin flies his kite and discovers electricity in lightning.

★ **Tip of the Week:**

If someone is coughing or gagging, you simply need to be polite, smile sympathetically, and offer water when it is over. (Water does nothing for choking, but it gives the choker some time to regain dignity.) The Heimlich can do harm if performed on someone who is not in need of it.

June

S	M	T	W	T	F	S
1	2	3	4	5	6	7
8	9	10	11	12	13	14
15	16	17	18	19	20	21
22	23	24	25	26	27	28
29	30					

HOW TO CROSS A PIRANHA-INFESTED RIVER

1 Do not cross if you have an open wound.
Piranhas are attracted to blood.

2 Avoid areas with netted fish, docks where fish are cleaned, and areas around bird rookeries.
Piranhas may become habituated to feeding in these areas and may be more aggressive there.

3 Stay out of the water when piranhas are feeding.
When large numbers of piranhas are attacking prey—a true feeding frenzy—they may snap and bite at anything around them. If you see them feeding, stay away, or well upriver.

4 Cross the river at night.
Virtually every species of piranha rests at night, and when awakened, will swim away rather than attack. Piranhas are most active at dawn, though some large adults may hunt in the evening.

5 Swim or walk across quickly and quietly.
Try not to create a large disturbance in the water that might awaken piranhas.

Piranhas are more active (and hungry) during the day, so cross an infested river at night.

JUNE

Monday **16**	Tuesday **17**	Wednesday **18**
	1867—Dr. Joseph Lister performs the first surgical operation under antiseptic conditions.	1983—Sally Ride becomes the first American woman in space.

Thursday **19**	Friday **20**	Saturday **21** *Last Quarter* ☽
		Summer Solstice
		Sunday **22**
2000—A fisherman is bitten by a piranha in a lake in Russia's Volga region. It is unknown how the South American fish got there.	1874—The first U.S. lifesaving medal is awarded.	1611—Explorer Henry Hudson, his son, and several others are set adrift by mutineers in the bay that will later bear his name.

★**Tip of the Week:**

Piranhas generally do not attack humans or large animals—unless they are already dead or injured. During the dry season, however, when their food supply is scarce, they can be more aggressive.

June

S	M	T	W	T	F	S
1	2	3	4	5	6	7
8	9	10	11	12	13	14
15	16	17	18	19	20	21
22	23	24	25	26	27	28
29	30					

HOW TO AVOID BEING STRUCK BY LIGHTNING

1 Loud or frequent thunder indicates that lightning activity is approaching. If you can see lightning and/or hear thunder, you are at risk. High winds, rainfall, and cloud cover often act as precursors to actual cloud-to-ground strikes.

2 When you see lightning, count the number of seconds until thunder is heard and then multiply by five. This will indicate how far the storm is from you in miles. (Sound travels at 1,100 feet per second.)

3 If the time delay between seeing the flash (lightning) and hearing the boom (thunder) is less than thirty seconds, seek a safer location immediately.

4 Avoid high places, open fields, and ridges above the timberline.

5 If in an open area, do not lie flat: kneel with your hands on the ground and your head low to make yourself less of a target.

If you are in an open area, do not lie flat. Kneel with your hands on the ground and your head low.

6 Avoid isolated trees, unprotected gazebos, and rain or picnic shelters, as well as shallow depressions in the earth: current traveling through the ground may use you to bridge the depression.

7 Wait for the storm to pass. The lightning threat generally diminishes with time after the last sound of thunder, but may persist for more than 30 minutes. When thunderstorms are in the area but not overhead, the lightning threat can exist even when it is sunny, not raining, or when clear sky is visible.

JUNE

Monday **23**	Tuesday **24**	Wednesday **25**
1860—The U.S. Secret Service is created.		1667—The first blood transfusion is administered.
Thursday **26**	Friday **27**	Saturday **28**
		1975—Golfer Lee Trevino is struck by lightning at the Western Open in Illinois.
		Sunday *New Moon* ● **29**
	1923—The first midair refueling between airplanes is completed near San Diego, California.	

★ **Tip of the Week:**

Large, enclosed buildings tend to be much safer than small or open structures. Fully enclosed metal vehicles such as cars, trucks, buses, vans, and enclosed farm vehicles with the windows rolled up provide good shelter from lightning. Avoid contact with metal or conducting surfaces outside or inside the vehicle.

June

S	M	T	W	T	F	S
1	2	3	4	5	6	7
8	9	10	11	12	13	14
15	16	17	18	19	20	21
22	23	24	25	26	27	28
29	30					

HOW TO SURVIVE A WILD ANIMAL BITE

- Immediately wash the bite out with soap and warm running water, if possible.

- Dress the wound with a sterile cloth or bandage. Put pressure on the wound to stop bleeding, if necessary.

- Capture the animal, if possible. If the animal is wild and you kill it, preserve its head: the brain will be tested for disease and viral infection (rabies). Do not freeze the animal or its head.

- If the animal is domestic and it has tags, contact the owner and write down the rabies tag number. The owner is responsible for quarantining the animal until it can be checked by a medical professional.

- If the animal cannot be captured, be prepared to give doctors and animal control authorities a description of the animal. Write down the type of animal, its size, color, behavior, any distinguishing marks, and the location and time of the attack.

- Get medical attention as soon as possible.

- Report the bite to animal control authorities.

JUNE/JULY

Monday
30

1859—Charles Blondin walks a tightrope across Niagara Falls.

Tuesday
1

Canada Day

Wednesday
2

Thursday
3

Friday
4

Independence Day

1776—The Declaration of Independence is signed.

Saturday
5

1810—P. T. Barnum is born.

Sunday
6

First Quarter ☽

1885—The first rabies shot is given by Louis Pasteur.

★ **Tip of the Week:**

If you cannot determine whether you have been infected with rabies due to a wild animal bite, you will need to undergo treatment. Symptoms of rabies develop within two to eight weeks after infection. Early symptoms include mental depression, restlessness, abnormal sensations such as itching around the site of the bite, headache, fever, tiredness, nausea, sore throat, or loss of appetite.

June						
S	M	T	W	T	F	S
1	2	3	4	5	6	7
8	9	10	11	12	13	14
15	16	17	18	19	20	21
22	23	24	25	26	27	28
29	30					

July						
S	M	T	W	T	F	S
		1	2	3	4	5
6	7	8	9	10	11	12
13	14	15	16	17	18	19
20	21	22	23	24	25	26
27	28	29	30	31		

HOW TO SURVIVE
A RIOT IN A FOREIGN COUNTRY

1 Remain indoors if you learn about any nearby rioting or civil unrest. Avoid the windows. Listen for reports on radio or television.

2 If you believe a crisis is unavoidable or seriously threatens your life, plan to leave the country as soon as possible.

3 Determine the best route to the airport or embassy, and sketch a map. Make sure that the airport is operating before you go. If you cannot make it to your own country's embassy, head for the embassy of an allied nation.

4 Wear clothing in muted tones so you do not stand out. Wear a long-sleeve shirt, jacket, jeans, a hat, socks, and lightweight boots.

5 Exit away from gunfire or mobs. Select a way out that is not easily observed. Ideal exits include windows, vents, or even the roof.

6 Leave as a group. You are safer with company when out in the open. Snipers or enemies will have multiple objects to focus on, not just one, and will not be as likely to make a move.

7 Do not run. Unless you believe your life is in imminent danger, walk. Running will generate excitement—people may chase you.

8 Drive a car if possible. Remember that a car can be a useful 2,000-pound weapon that even a mob cannot stop. Drive on back streets, not main roads, and be prepared to abandon the car if the situation becomes critical.

9 Get to the airport or an embassy as quickly as possible.

JULY

Monday
7

Annual Event: The festival of San Fermin (the Running of the Bulls) takes place all week in Pamplona, Spain.

1891—Traveler's checks are patented by American Express.

Tuesday
8

Wednesday
9

Thursday
10

Friday
11

Saturday
12

1798—U.S. Marine Corps is created by an act of Congress.

Sunday   *Full Moon* ○
13

1898—Guglielmo Marconi patents the radio.

★ **Tip of the Week:**

When in a volatile region where civil disorder is a likelihood, always keep a small bag handy with the following supplies: flashlight, small compass, detailed map of the city, knife, fire-starting tool, black garbage bags, water and food, money, passports, and official documents for your family.

July

S	M	T	W	T	F	S
		1	2	3	4	5
6	7	8	9	10	11	12
13	14	15	16	17	18	19
20	21	22	23	24	25	26
27	28	29	30	31		

HOW TO SURVIVE A NUCLEAR EXPLOSION

1 An underground shelter covered by one meter or more of earth will provide the best protection against a nuclear explosion and fallout radiation.
However, if you cannot get to such a shelter, the following structures offer the next best protection:
- Caves or tunnels covered by more than one meter of earth
- Storm or storage cellars
- Basements
- Abandoned buildings made of stone or mud

2 If you have been exposed to radiation, immediately wash your body thoroughly with soap and water, even if the water may also be contaminated. This will remove most of the radiation particles, but not all. If no water is available, wipe yourself down with a clean cloth or uncontaminated dirt (dirt that is at least a meter under the surface).

3 You can safely obtain water from underground sources (springs and wells, for example) that undergo natural filtration, or from pipes in abandoned houses or stores.
Snow that you take from 15 or more centimeters below the surface is also a safe source of water.

4 Even though wild animals may not be free from contamination, you can use them as a food source if other foods are not available.
Do not, however, eat an animal that appears to be sick. Carefully skin all animals, and do not eat meat close to the bones and joints (an animal's skeleton contains over 90 percent of the radioactivity). All eggs, even if laid during the period of fallout, will be safe to eat.

JULY

Monday **14**	Tuesday **15**	Wednesday **16**
1977—New York City regains power after a 25-hour blackout.	1916—The Boeing Company is founded in Seattle.	1945—The first atomic bomb is tested in New Mexico.

Thursday **17**	Friday **18**	Saturday **19**
		Sunday **20**
1989—The first stealth bomber is tested in Area 51.		1969—Neil Armstrong sets foot on the moon.

★ **Tip of the Week:**

After a nuclear explosion, you will need to get to a safe shelter and remain inside for four to six days. Limit your surface exposure to no more than thirty minutes until thirteen days have passed. After the thirteenth day, it is probably safe to emerge more frequently, but keep your exposure brief.

July

S	M	T	W	T	F	S
		1	2	3	4	5
6	7	8	9	10	11	12
13	14	15	16	17	18	19
20	21	22	23	24	25	26
27	28	29	30	31		

THE *ANDREA DORIA* AND THE *STOCKHOLM* COLLIDE

On the foggy night of July 25, 1956, the Italian passenger ship *Andrea Doria* slowly made its way toward port. Meanwhile, the Swedish cruise ship *Stockholm* had left New York on a course that would pass near the shores of Nantucket.

When the ships came within seventeen miles of each other, blips appeared on the radars. Both ships adjusted their courses, but soon, the crew of the *Andrea Doria* was able to spot the *Stockholm*—only a few miles away.

The ships could have still passed safely, but the *Stockholm*'s captain misread his radar, believing the other ship to be six miles away when the difference was actually two. The crew of the *Andrea Doria* watched, horrified, as the *Stockholm* pierced their ship deeply through the middle. The "unsinkable" ship had been hit at its most vulnerable spot, and the ship immediately began listing steeply.

Half the lifeboats were rendered useless due to the listing, but the few that could be used were quickly dropped. All the while, the captain radioed S.O.S. distress signals to other ships. The first to arrive was the *Ile de France*, which was able to rescue the majority of the passengers.

The next morning, the *Andrea Doria* rolled over, completely capsized. It was one of the worst passenger ship sea collisions in history, but it was also the greatest sea rescue of all time—1660 of the 1706 passengers and crew were rescued.

JULY

Monday
Last Quarter ☽
21

1899—Ernest Hemingway is born.

Tuesday
22

Wednesday
23

Thursday
24

1987—91-year-old Hulda Crooks climbs Mount Fuji in Japan.

Friday
25

1956—The *Andrea Doria* and the *Stockholm* collide in dense fog.

Saturday
26

1908—The B.O.I., later renamed the F.B.I., is created.

Sunday
27

★ **Tip of the Week:**

In a modern sea rescue, you may be rescued from your lifeboat or sinking ship by a helicopter. To avoid an electric shock, let the winch line touch the water before touching it. Then put the winch loop under your armpits and cross your arms. The helicopter will lift you to safety this way.

July

S	M	T	W	T	F	S
		1	2	3	4	5
6	7	8	9	10	11	12
13	14	15	16	17	18	19
20	21	22	23	24	25	26
27	28	29	30	31		

HOW TO SURVIVE A SANDSTORM

1 Wet a bandanna or other cloth and place it over your nose and mouth.

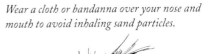
Wear a cloth or bandanna over your nose and mouth to avoid inhaling sand particles.

2 Use a small amount of petroleum jelly to coat your nostrils on the inside. The lubricant will help to minimize the drying of mucous membranes.

3 If on foot, all members of your group should stay together.
Link arms or use a rope to avoid becoming separated during the storm and to keep track of group members who might become injured or incapacitated.

4 If driving in a car, pull off the road as far as possible on the shoulder.
Turn off your lights, set the emergency brake, and make sure your taillights are not illuminated. (Vehicles approaching from the rear may inadvertently leave the road and collide with your parked car, thinking it's another vehicle traveling on the road.)

5 Try to move to higher ground.
Sand grains travel across the surface of the earth mostly by saltation, or bouncing from place to place. Because grains of sand will not bounce high on grass, dirt, or sand, moving to solid, high ground is advisable, even if it's just a few feet higher. However, sandstorms can be accompanied by severe thunderstorms, and there may be a risk of lightning. If you hear thunder or see lightning during a sandstorm, do not move to higher ground.

JULY/AUGUST

Monday *New Moon* ● # 28	**Tuesday** # 29	**Wednesday** # 30 1947—Arnold Schwarzenegger is born.
Thursday # 31	**Friday** # 1	**Saturday** # 2 1932—Peter O'Toole, star of *Lawrence of Arabia*, is born.
		Sunday # 3

1774—Oxygen is discovered.

★ **Tip of the Week:**

Whenever you are in an area with sandstorm potential (anywhere that there is a lot of sand and wind), wear long pants, socks, and shoes. Because of the way sand moves, your feet and lower legs are more likely to be "burned" by the abrasion of sand than the upper part of your body.

July

S	M	T	W	T	F	S
		1	2	3	4	5
6	7	8	9	10	11	12
13	14	15	16	17	18	19
20	21	22	23	24	25	26
27	28	29	30	31		

August

S	M	T	W	T	F	S
					1	2
3	4	5	6	7	8	9
10	11	12	13	14	15	16
17	18	19	20	21	22	23
24/31	25	26	27	28	29	30

HOW TO SURVIVE
IN FRIGID WATER

1 Do not attempt to swim unless it is for a very short distance.
A strong swimmer has a 50-50 chance of surviving a 50-yard swim in 50-degree Fahrenheit water. Swim only if you can reach land, a boat, or a floating object with a few strokes. Swimming moves cold water over skin, causing rapid cooling.

2 If you are wearing a flotation device, assume the Heat Escape Lessening Posture (HELP).
Cross your ankles, draw your knees to your chest, and cross your arms over your chest. Your hands should be kept high on your chest or neck to keep them warm. Do not remove clothing. Clothes will not weigh you down but will hold warm water against your skin like a diver's wetsuit. This position can reduce heat loss by 50 percent.

3 If two or more people are in the water and all are wearing flotation devices, assume the "huddle" position.
Two to four people should "hug," with chest touching chest. This position allows body heat to be shared. Also, rescuers can spot groups more easily than individuals.

Assume the "huddle" position to share body heat.

4 Keep movement to a minimum.
Increasing the heart rate speeds body cooling. Try to breathe normally.

5 Once you are rescued, watch for signs of hypothermia.
Slurred speech and a lack of shivering are signs of severe body temperature loss. Immediately rewarm your body in a warm water bath (100–105°F), keeping extremities out of the water, or use the body heat of another person to rewarm. Do not rub extremities in an attempt to warm them; tissue damage could occur.

AUGUST

Monday	Tuesday	Wednesday
## 4	## 5 *First Quarter* ☾	## 6

1958—The U.S. atomic submarine *Nautilus* completes the first undersea crossing of the North Pole, surfacing after 96 hours under a 50-foot-thick ice cap.

1926—Gertrude Ederle becomes the first woman to swim the English Channel.

Thursday	Friday	Saturday
## 7	## 8	## 9

1988—An ice hole fishing plug is patented.

Sunday
10

★ **Tip of the Week:**

If you are not wearing a flotation device, find something—a piece of driftwood or floating cooler—to use as a flotation device. Float on your back or try to assume the HELP position.

August

S	M	T	W	T	F	S
					1	2
3	4	5	6	7	8	9
10	11	12	13	14	15	16
17	18	19	20	21	22	23
24/31	25	26	27	28	29	30

HOW TO PERFORM
A TRACHEOTOMY

WHAT YOU WILL NEED:

- A first aid kit, if available
- A razor blade or very sharp knife
- A straw (two would be better) or a ballpoint pen
  with the inside (ink-filled tube) removed. If neither
  a straw nor a pen is available, use stiff paper or
  cardboard rolled into a tube. Good first-aid kits
  may contain "trache" tubes.

(There will not be time for sterilization of your tools,
so do not bother; infection is the least of your worries
at this point.)

1 Find the person's Adam's apple (thyroid cartilage).

2 Move your finger about one inch down the neck
until you feel another bulge.
This is the cricoid cartilage. The indentation between
the two is the cricothyroid membrane, where the incision will be made.

3 Take the razor blade or knife and make a one-
to two-centimeter (about half an inch) horizontal
incision.
The cut should be about half an inch deep. There
should not be too much blood.

4 Pinch the incision or insert your finger inside the
slit to open it.

5 Insert your tube into the incision, roughly one-half
to one inch deep.

Adam's apple

cricoid cartilage

1.

2.

3.

4.

AUGUST

Monday *Full Moon* ○	Tuesday	Wednesday
# 11	# 12	# 13
	1865—First use of disinfectant in surgery by Dr. Joseph Lister.	

Thursday	Friday	Saturday
# 14	# 15	# 16
		Sunday
		# 17
	1620—The *Mayflower* sets sail. 1888—T. E. Lawrence, a.k.a. Lawrence of Arabia, is born.	

★ Tip of the Week:

A tracheotomy, technically called a cricothyroidotomy, should be undertaken only when a person with a throat obstruction is not able to breathe at all—no gasping sounds, no coughing—and only after you have attempted to perform the Heimlich maneuver three times without dislodging the obstruction. If possible, someone should be calling for paramedics while you proceed.

August

S	M	T	W	T	F	S
					1	2
3	4	5	6	7	8	9
10	11	12	13	14	15	16
17	18	19	20	21	22	23
24/31	25	26	27	28	29	30

HOW TO SURVIVE A TSUNAMI

A tsunami (tidal wave) is a series of traveling ocean waves of extremely long length generated by geological disturbances such as earthquakes occurring below or near the ocean floor, underwater volcanic eruptions, and landslides. They have been known to range from 50 to 100 feet in height.

1 Be aware of the warning signs of an approaching tsunami:
- Rise or fall in sea level
- Shaking ground
- Loud, sustained roar

If you notice any of these signs, do not wait for a tsunami warning to be announced. Stay away from rivers and streams that lead to the ocean: tsunamis can travel up these bodies of water.

2 If you are on a boat in a small harbor and you have sufficient warning of an approaching tsunami, you may want to move your boat into open water, away from shore.
Be aware that rough seas may present a greater hazard to life and limb than a tsunami, especially if there is time to reach high ground.

3 If you are on land, move to higher ground immediately.
Tsunamis can move faster than a person can run. Get away from the coastline as quickly as possible.

4 If you are in a high-rise hotel or apartment building on the coastline and you do not have enough time to get to a higher location away from shore, move to a high floor of the building.
The upper floors of a high rise building can provide safe refuge.

AUGUST

Monday
18

1896—Davy Crockett is born.

Tuesday
19

Last Quarter ☾

Wednesday
20

1957—U.S. Air Force Major David G. Simons sets a record for balloon ascent and longest stay on the edge of space by rising to (and hovering at) 101,485 feet.

Thursday
21

1912—The first Eagle Scout, Arthur R. Eldred, is awarded the highest rank in the Boy Scouts.

Friday
22

Saturday
23

Sunday
24

79 C.E.—Mt. Vesuvius erupts on Pompeii.

1992—Hurricane Andrew hits the coast of Florida, devastating Miami.

★ **Tip of the Week:**

The first tsunami wave may not be the largest in the series of waves. One coastal community may see no damaging wave activity while in another, waves can be large and violent. Moreover, the flooding can extend inland by 1,000 feet or more, covering large expanses of land with water and debris.

August

S	M	T	W	T	F	S
					1	2
3	4	5	6	7	8	9
10	11	12	13	14	15	16
17	18	19	20	21	22	23
24/31	25	26	27	28	29	30

HOW TO SURVIVE WHEN LOST IN THE MOUNTAINS

1 Do not panic.
If you told someone where you were going, search and rescue teams will be looking for you. (In general, teams will search only during daylight hours for adults, but will search around the clock for children who are alone.)

2 Find shelter, and stay warm and dry.
Exerting yourself unnecessarily—like dragging heavy logs to build a shelter—will make you sweat and make you cold. Use the shelter around you before trying to construct one.

3 Signal rescuers for help.
The best time to signal rescuers is during the day, with a signaling device or three fires in a triangle. Signal for help from the highest point possible—it will be easier for rescuers to see you, and any sound you make will travel further. Build three smoky fires and put your blanket—gold side facing out if it is a space blanket—on the ground.

In snow-covered country, build a snow cave or a snow trench for shelter and warmth. Use dead leaves and branches for insulation.

4 Do not wander far.
It will make finding you more difficult, as search teams will be trying to retrace your path and may miss you if you have gone off in a different direction. Searchers often wind up finding a vehicle with no one in it because the driver has wandered off.

AUGUST

Monday	Tuesday	Wednesday *New Moon* ●
25	**26**	**27**
1916—The National Park Service is established as part of the U.S. Department of the Interior.	1346—The first use of artillery in battle.	1966—Sir Francis Chichester embarks on the first solo boat voyage around the world.

Thursday	Friday	Saturday
28	**29**	**30**
		1929—The submarine "lung" is tested by the U.S. Navy.

Sunday

31

★ **Tip of the Week:**

Always carry something that you can use as a signal device should you need it. A small mirror works well, as do flares, a whistle, and even newspaper (which stands out against the ground) or aluminum foil.

August

S	M	T	W	T	F	S
					1	2
3	4	5	6	7	8	9
10	11	12	13	14	15	16
17	18	19	20	21	22	23
24/31	25	26	27	28	29	30

HOW TO ESCAPE FROM QUICKSAND

When walking in quicksand country, carry a stout pole—it will help you get out should you need to.

1 As soon as you start to sink, lay the pole on the surface of the quicksand.

2 Do not struggle, and move slowly. Quicksand is not difficult to float in—but it can suck you down if you struggle too hard against it.

3 Flop onto your back on top of the pole. After a minute or two, equilibrium in the quicksand will be achieved, and you will no longer sink.

When in an area with quicksand, bring a stout pole and use it to put your back into a floating position.

Place the pole at a right angle to your spine to keep your hips afloat.

4 Work the pole to a new position: under your hips, and at a right angle to your spine. The pole will keep your hips from sinking as you (slowly) pull out first one leg, and then the other.

5 Take the shortest route to firmer ground, moving slowly.

SEPTEMBER

Monday
1
Labor Day

Tuesday
2
1901—Teddy Roosevelt advises, "Speak softly and carry a big stick."

Wednesday
3
First Quarter ☾

Thursday
4
1965—"Help" by the Beatles goes to #1 on *Billboard*'s Top 40.

Friday
5

Saturday
6
1522—Ferdinand Magellan's ship, *Victoria*, completes the first curcumnavigation of the globe.

Sunday
7
1987—A two-day operation to separate infant twins joined at the head is completed successfully at Johns Hopkins in Baltimore.

★ **Tip of the Week:**

Floating on quicksand is relatively easy and is the best way to avoid its clutches. You are more buoyant in quicksand than you are in water. If you do not have a pole, spread your arms and legs far apart and try to float on your back.

September

S	M	T	W	T	F	S
		1	2	3	4	5	6
7	8	9	10	11	12	13
14	15	16	17	18	19	20
21	22	23	24	25	26	27
28	29	30				

HOW TO CATCH
FISH WITHOUT A ROD

1 Determine the best location for your fishing. Fish usually congregate in shadows, and near the edges of lakes, rivers, and streams.

2 Find a forked sapling branch approximately two feet long.
The forked ends should be approximately one foot long each.

Find a forked branch. Tie the ends together.

3 Bend the two ends toward each other and tie them together.
This will form the circular frame of a net.

4 Remove your shirt or undershirt.

Tie a shirt into a knot.

5 Tie a knot in the shirt just before the arm and neck holes.

6 Slip the branch into the shirt, and pin or tie the shirt securely to the frame.

7 Scoop up the fish.

Slip the branch into the shirt; secure the shirt to the frame.

SEPTEMBER

Monday
8

1953—Ernest Hemingway's
The Old Man and the Sea is published.

Tuesday
9

1904—Mounted police are used for
the first time in New York City.

Wednesday
10

Full Moon ○

1913—Lincoln Highway opens as the
first coast-to-coast highway.

Thursday
11

Friday
12

Saturday
13

1970—126 runners start and 55 finish
the first New York City Marathon.

Sunday
14

★ **Tip of the Week:**

Large fish can also be speared with a pole sharpened to a point at one end.
This method works best at night, when fish come to the surface.

September

S	M	T	W	T	F	S
	1	2	3	4	5	6
7	8	9	10	11	12	13
14	15	16	17	18	19	20
21	22	23	24	25	26	27
28	29	30				

HOW TO SURVIVE IF YOU ARE ATTACKED BY LEECHES

1 Do not attempt to remove a leech by pulling up on its middle section or by using salt, heat, or insect repellent.
Dislodging by squeezing, salting, burning, or otherwise annoying the leech while it is feeding will cause it to regurgitate, most likely spreading the bacteria from its digestive system into your open wound, causing infection.

2 Identify the anterior (oral) sucker.
Look for the small end of the leech. A common mistake is to go immediately to the large sucker.

3 Place a fingernail on your skin (not on the leech itself), directly adjacent to the oral sucker.

4 Gently but firmly slide your finger toward where the leech is feeding and push the sucker away sideways.
When the seal made by the oral sucker is broken, the leech will stop feeding. After the oral sucker has been dislodged, the leech's head will seek to reattach, and it may attach to the finger that displaced the head. Even if the oral sucker attaches again, the leech does not begin to feed immediately.

5 Displace the posterior (hind) sucker.
While continuing to flick occasionally at the head end, push at or pick under the hind sucker with a fingernail to cause it to lose its suction.

6 Dispose of the leech.
Once the leech is detached, you can put salt or insect repellent directly on it to keep it from attaching to anything else.

7 Treat the wound.
Keep the area clean, and cover it with a small bandage if necessary. If itching becomes severe, take an antihistamine.

SEPTEMBER

Monday
15

Tuesday
16

1984—The first successful transplant of an animal heart (baboon) into a human being.

Wednesday
17

1967—The TV show *Mission: Impossible* premieres on CBS.

Thursday   *Last Quarter* ☽
18

Friday
19

1911—William Golding, author of *Lord of the Flies*, is born.

Saturday
20

1519—Ferdinand Magellan sets out on his voyage to circumnavigate the world.

Sunday
21

1947—Stephen King, author of *The Body*, the inspiration for the film *Stand by Me*, is born.

★ **Tip of the Week:**

Leeches need a solid surface to hold onto even when they are not feeding. Avoid leeches by staying in the open: swim in deep, open water, avoid boat docks, and do not wade through areas with submerged branches or rocks. In jungles, remain on trails and be aware of leeches on overhanging branches and vines.

September

S	M	T	W	T	F	S
		1	2	3	4	5	6
7	8	9	10	11	12	13
14	15	16	17	18	19	20
21	22	23	24	25	26	27
28	29	30				

HOW TO SURVIVE A RIPTIDE

Riptides are long, narrow bands of water that quickly pull any objects in them away from shore and out to sea. Riptides are different from undertow, however, which pulls you underwater. Riptides or rip currents are dangerous, but they are relatively easy to escape, as long as you follow these steps.

1 Do not panic.

2 Do not swim in toward shore.
You will be fighting the current, and you will lose.

3 Swim parallel to shore, across the current, to escape.
Generally, a riptide is less than 100 feet wide, so swimming beyond it should not be too difficult.

4 If you cannot swim out of the riptide, float on your back and allow the riptide to take you away from shore until it disappears.
Rip currents generally subside 50 to 100 yards from shore. Then swim sideways and back to shore.

(Direction of rip current)

To escape a rip current, swim parallel to shore until you are beyond the pull of the rip current.

SEPTEMBER

Monday **22**	Tuesday **23**	Wednesday **24**
1921—The Band-Aid is patented.	Equinox	1929—The first "blind" airplane flight, in which the pilot used only instruments to navigate, is completed in Mitchell Field, New York, by Lt. James H. Doolittle.

Thursday *New Moon* ● **25**	Friday **26**	Saturday **27**
		Rosh Hashanah
1998—Ben Lecomte of France becomes the first person to swim across the Atlantic Ocean.		Sunday **28**

★ Tip of the Week:

To spot a rip current:

- Know that they can occur more frequently in strong winds.
- Look for streaks of muddy or sandy water and floating debris moving out to sea through the surf zone.
- Look for areas of reduced wave heights in the surf zone.
- Look for depressions in the beach running perpendicular to shore.

September

S	M	T	W	T	F	S
	1	2	3	4	5	6
7	8	9	10	11	12	13
14	15	16	17	18	19	20
21	22	23	24	25	26	27
28	29	30				

HOW TO USE A DEFIBRILLATOR TO RESTORE A HEARTBEAT

1 Turn on the defibrillator by pressing the green button.
Most machines will provide both visual and voice prompts.

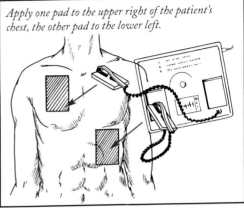

Apply one pad to the upper right of the patient's chest, the other pad to the lower left.

2 Remove the person's shirt and jewelry, then apply the pads to the chest as shown on the machine's LED panel.
One pad should be placed on the upper right side of the patient's chest, one on the lower left.

3 Plug the pads into the connector.
The defibrillator will analyze the patient and determine if he or she needs a shock. Do not touch the patient at this time.

4 If the machine determines that a shock is needed, it will direct you to press the orange button to deliver a shock.
Do not touch the patient after pressing the button. The machine will automatically check to see whether or not the patient needs a second shock and, if so, will direct you to press the orange button again.

5 Check the patient's airway, breathing, and pulse.
If there is a pulse but the patient is not breathing, begin mouth-to-mouth resuscitation. If there is no pulse, repeat the defibrillation process.

SEPTEMBER/OCTOBER

Monday	Tuesday	Wednesday
29	**30**	**1**
	1882—The first hydroelectric power plant opens.	

Thursday *First Quarter* ☽	Friday	Saturday
2	**3**	**4**
		1957—*Sputnik 1* is launched by the U.S.S.R.

		Sunday
		5
1869—Mohandas K. Gandhi is born. 1937—The first successful moving picture X-ray of the heart is exhibited.		1931—Hugh Herndon and Clyde Pangborn complete the first nonstop flight across the Pacific.

★ **Tip of the Week:**

A defibrillator should be used for a person experiencing Sudden Cardiac Arrest (SCA), a condition where the heart's electrical signals become confused and the heart ceases to function properly. The defibrillator will assess whether or not a shock is needed—if it is not, try CPR.

September

S	M	T	W	T	F	S
	1	2	3	4	5	6
7	8	9	10	11	12	13
14	15	16	17	18	19	20
21	22	23	24	25	26	27
28	29	30				

October

S	M	T	W	T	F	S
			1	2	3	4
5	6	7	8	9	10	11
12	13	14	15	16	17	18
19	20	21	22	23	24	25
26	27	28	29	30	31	

HOW TO RAM YOUR CAR THROUGH A BARRICADE

1 Identify the barricade's weakest point.
The side of the barricade that opens, or the place where a lock holds it closed, is usually its most vulnerable spot.

2 Aim for the weak spot.
If possible, use the rear of the car to ram the weak spot—hitting with the front may damage the engine and cause the car to stall.

3 Step on the gas and accelerate to a speed of 30 to 45 mph.
Traveling any faster will cause unnecessary damage to the car. Keep your foot on the gas all the way through. Consider how much room you will need to turn or stop once you clear the barricade.

4 Duck just before impact if you are heading toward an extremely tall barricade or fence.
Pieces of the barricade may break through the window.

5 Avoid poles or anchors in the ground.
These may bend and not break, and then drag against and damage the underside of the car, preventing you from driving.

6 Repeat as necessary to break through.

Aim for the weakest part of the barricade—often where the lock is.

OCTOBER

Monday	Tuesday	Wednesday
# 6	# 7	# 8
Yom Kippur		1871—The Chicago Fire begins—it will take firefighters three days to put out the blaze.

Thursday	Friday *Full Moon* ○	Saturday
# 9	# 10	# 11
		1984—Dr. Kathryn D. Sullivan becomes the first U.S. woman to walk in space.

Sunday
12
Columbus Day

1959—Pan American World Airways announces the first passenger service to circle the globe.

1971—Dr. Allan M. Cormack and Geoffrey Hounsfield are awarded the Nobel Prize in medicine for developing the CAT scan.

★ **Tip of the Week:**

For electrically-powered gates that swing open and closed (like those found in gated communities and apartment complexes), it is better to push the gate open than to ram it. If you are traveling in the direction the gate opens, simply ease your bumper up to and against the gate. Your car will easily overpower the small electric motor that operates the gate.

October

S	M	T	W	T	F	S
			1	2	3	4
5	6	7	8	9	10	11
12	13	14	15	16	17	18
19	20	21	22	23	24	25
26	27	28	29	30	31	

HOW TO ESCAPE FROM THE TRUNK OF A CAR

1 If you are in a trunk that is up against the backseat of the car, try to get the seats down.
Although the release for most seats is inside the passenger compartment, you may be able to fold or force them down from the trunk side.

2 Check for a trunk cable underneath the carpet or upholstery.
Many new cars have a trunk release inside the passenger compartment of the car. These cars should have a cable that runs from the release to the trunk latch. Look behind carpeting or upholstery, or behind a panel of sheet metal.

3 Pull on the cable to release the trunk latch.

4 If you cannot find a cable release, look for a tool in the trunk.
Many cars have emergency kits inside the trunk, underneath or with the spare tire. These kits may contain a screwdriver, flashlight, or pry bar.

5 Use a screwdriver or pry bar to pry the latch open.
You can also pry the corner of the trunk lid up and yell to signal passersby.

If the trunk has a cable release, pull on it to release the latch.

6 If you cannot find a tool inside, dismantle the car's brake lights by yanking wires and pushing or kicking the lights out.
Then wave and yell to signal passersby or other cars. This method is also recommended if the car is moving and you need to signal cars behind you.

OCTOBER

Monday **13**	Tuesday **14**	Wednesday **15**
Columbus Day Observed Canadian Thanksgiving	1947—Chuck Yeager breaks the sound barrier.	

Thursday **16**	Friday **17**	Saturday *Last Quarter* ☽ **18**
		Sunday **19**
1987—Baby Jessica McClure is rescued from a well in Midland, Texas. 1987—A three-hour-old baby becomes the youngest person ever to undergo a heart transplant.	2000—The Department of Transportation announces that internal latch releases will be mandatory in all future automobile trunks.	

★ **Tips of the Week:**
- Don't panic. No car trunk is airtight, so the danger of suffocation in a car trunk is low.
- On a hot day the interior temperature of a car trunk can reach 140 degrees, and hundreds of heat-related deaths have been recorded. Work quickly but calmly if trapped in the trunk on a hot day.

October

S	M	T	W	T	F	S
			1	2	3	4
5	6	7	8	9	10	11
12	13	14	15	16	17	18
19	20	21	22	23	24	25
26	27	28	29	30	31	

HOW TO SURVIVE IF YOUR PARACHUTE FAILS TO OPEN

1 Signal to a jumping companion that you're having a malfunction.
Wave your arms and point to your chute.

2 When your companion (and new best friend) gets to you, hook arms.

> *Hook arms with your companion. Then hook your arms into his chest strap, up to the elbows, and grab hold of your own.*

3 Once you are hooked together, the two of you will still be falling at terminal velocity, about 130 mph. When your friend opens his chute, there will be no way either of you will be able to hold onto one another normally, because the G-forces will triple or quadruple your body weight. To combat this, hook your arms into his chest strap, or through the two sides of the front of his harness, all the way up to your elbows. Then grab hold of your own harness.

4 Open the chute.

5 The chute opening shock will be severe, probably enough to dislocate or break your arms.
Your friend now must hold on to you with one arm while steering his canopy (the part of the chute that controls direction and speed).

6 If your friend's canopy is slow and big, you may hit the grass or dirt slowly enough to break only a leg, and your chances of survival are high.

7 If there is a body of water nearby, head for that.
Once you hit the water, you will have to tread with just your legs, and hope that your partner is able to pull you out.

OCTOBER

Monday
20

1911—Norwegian explorer Roald Amundsen sets out for the South Pole.

Tuesday
21

Wednesday
22

1797—The first parachute jump is performed from a balloon by Andre-Jacques Garnerin, the inventor of the parachute.

Thursday
23

Friday
24

United Nations Day

1901—The first person jumps over Niagara Falls in a barrel.

1945—The United Nations is officially established.

Saturday   *New Moon* ●
25

1854—The famous "Charge of the Light Brigade" takes place, marking the most disastrous campaign of the Crimean War.

Sunday
26

★ **Tip of the Week:**

Check your chute before you jump. Make sure that the parachute is folded in straight lines—that there are no twists—and that the slider is positioned correctly to keep the parachute from opening too fast. The good news is that today's parachutes are built to open, so even if you make big mistakes packing them, they tend to sort themselves out.

October

S	M	T	W	T	F	S
			1	2	3	4
5	6	7	8	9	10	11
12	13	14	15	16	17	18
19	20	21	22	23	24	25
26	27	28	29	30	31	

HOW TO SURVIVE
A FALL ONTO SUBWAY TRACKS

1 Do not attempt to climb back onto the platform unless you are positive you have enough time to do so.

2 Find a safe place to stand, out of the way of oncoming trains. Avoid areas of the ground near the track and the walls that are marked with a strip of tape or with red and white painted stripes. These markings indicate that the train passes extremely close to these areas, and you will not have enough clearance.

Between columns

Beneath Platform

Opposite Track

Inside Alcove

If you fall onto the tracks, head for these areas.

3 Stand in one of the following areas, in order of preference:
- Against a wall
- Between columns separating two tracks
- On an adjoining set of tracks
- Beneath the platform

4 Remove any articles of clothing or bags that could catch on the train, and stand straight, still, and tall.

5 Immediately after a train has passed, quickly climb back onto the platform.

OCTOBER/NOVEMBER

Monday
27

1904—The Manhattan subway opens.

Tuesday
28

1929—The first recorded birth of a baby in an airplane.

Wednesday
29

Thursday
30

1939—Orson Welles causes panic when he broadcasts his famous "War of the Worlds."

Friday
31

First Quarter ☽

Halloween

Saturday
1

Sunday
2

1734—Daniel Boone is born.

★ **Tip of the Week:**

If there are no obvious alcoves or recessed spots to go to and a train is approaching, and there is a depression in the concrete between the rails, lie down in it—there will be enough room for the train to pass over you. (Use this method only in desperation—the train may be dragging something, or there may not be clearance.)

October

S	M	T	W	T	F	S
			1	2	3	4
5	6	7	8	9	10	11
12	13	14	15	16	17	18
19	20	21	22	23	24	25
26	27	28	29	30	31	

November

S	M	T	W	T	F	S
						1
2	3	4	5	6	7	8
9	10	11	12	13	14	15
16	17	18	19	20	21	22
23/30	24	25	26	27	28	29

HOW TO ESCAPE A BAD DATE

1 Locate an exit.
Do not open an emergency exit if it is alarmed unless absolutely necessary; an alarm will only draw attention to you.

2 If there are no accessible doors, locate a usable window.
Avoid windows with chicken wire or large plate glass. Bathroom windows work best. If you are not on the ground floor, be sure there is a fire escape.

3 Attempt to open the window.

4 If you cannot open the window, find an implement you can use to break it.
Suitable implements are wastebaskets, toilet plungers, or toilet brushes.

5 Strike the center of the glass.
If the hand holding the implement will come within a foot of the window as you break it, wrap it with a jacket or sweater before attempting to break the glass. If no implement is available, use your heavily wrapped hand; be sure you wrap your arm as well, beyond the elbow.

6 Punch out any remaining shards of glass.
Cover your fist with a jacket or sweater before removing the glass.

7 Make your escape.
Do not worry about any minor nicks and cuts. Just run.

If the window does not open, attempt to break it with a hard implement, such as a wastebasket.

NOVEMBER

Monday	Tuesday	Wednesday
3	**4**	**5**
1957—The first animal is launched into space by the U.S.S.R.	**Election Day**	

Thursday	Friday	Saturday *Full Moon* ○
6	**7**	**8**
		1805—Lewis and Clark reach the Pacific Ocean.

Sunday
9
1938—The first Sadie Hawkins Day is held.

★**Tip of the Week:**

Instead of making a getaway, you can attempt to coerce your date to leave. Try saying something offensive, behaving inappropriately, or sending your date on a fool's errand.

November

S	M	T	W	T	F	S
						1
2	3	4	5	6	7	8
9	10	11	12	13	14	15
16	17	18	19	20	21	22
23/30	24	25	26	27	28	29

TWO WOMEN SKI ACROSS ANTARCTICA

On November 13, 2000, two former schoolteachers—45-year-old American Ann Bancroft and 47-year-old Norwegian Liv Arnesen—began their attempt to become the first women to ski across Antarctica unaided. The route totaled 2,400 miles across barren terrain in temperatures averaging -30°F.

Rigged with sails to pull them at speeds up to 25 mph, each hauled a 267-pound sled. On January 16, 2001, the women reached the South Pole and stopped to refresh, having endured 64 days of rough weather, including whiteouts and lack of wind. They had covered nearly 1,300 miles, were three weeks behind schedule, and were low on rations, subsisting primarily on chocolate bars and oatmeal.

With 1,000 miles to go, the women triumphantly set out, but the traveling was brutal. At Shackleton's Glacier, sharp blue ice broke spikes off their crampons (iron-spiked shoes) and slashed a three-foot gash in a sled. The pair had to backtrack up the glacier to get out, losing valuable time. On the final leg of the journey, the crossing of the Ross Ice Shelf, winds died down to nothing. They were still 500 miles from the other coast.

After three windless days on the Ross Ice Shelf, the women reluctantly decided to call for an airlift. Though they did not reach their goal, they came closer to it than any women before them. Together they fought the elements, managing to walk in the footsteps of great heroes like Ernest Shackleton. In every way, they are survivors.

NOVEMBER

Monday **10**	Tuesday **11**	Wednesday **12**
1885—The first motorcycle ride is taken by Paul Daimler, son of its inventor.	Veterans Day Remembrance Day (Canada)	1933—The first reported sighting of the Loch Ness Monster.

Thursday **13**	Friday **14**	Saturday **15**
		1922—Dr. Alexis Carrel announces his discovery of white blood cells, which prevent the spread of infection.
1927—The Holland Tunnel (the first underwater motor vehicle tunnel in the U.S.) opens to commercial traffic between New Jersey and Manhattan. 2000—Liv Arnesen and Ann Bancroft set out to ski across Antarctica.		Sunday *Last Quarter* ☽ **16**

★ **Tip of the Week:**

To avoid frostbite when traveling in bitterly cold areas, periodically wrinkle your face to prevent stiff patches from forming.

November

S	M	T	W	T	F	S
						1
2	3	4	5	6	7	8
9	10	11	12	13	14	15
16	17	18	19	20	21	22
23/30	24	25	26	27	28	29

PLANTS YOU CAN EAT

Hundreds of plant species are edible, though some require preparation to make them digestible and/or palatable. Here are five you can eat:

- **BLACK WALNUTS**—These look like commercial walnuts after you remove them from their green husks. Stomp off the husk with your shoe, then crack the nut with a heavy rock. Can be eaten raw or cooked.
- **BURDOCK**—This plant has huge, wedge-shaped leaves that are whitish underneath. Scrub the first-year taproot, cut it into razor-thin diagonal slices, and cook over open flame for 10–20 minutes. (The second year, the roots are too tough to eat.) You can also peel the tender, immature flowerstalk in late spring and cook it.
- **DANDELIONS**—Among the most widespread and common edible plants. You can eat the leaves raw or cook them.
- **MULBERRIES**—These look like raspberries, but each delicious berry has a slender stem. Harvest them in quantity by shaking the tree's branches over a dropcloth.
- **WILD ONIONS**—These plants have leaves that look like chives or scallions and smell like onions and garlic. The bulbs are much smaller than their commercial relatives, but you can use the leaves and bulbs as you would a commercial onion. Be aware that some wild onion look-alikes are poisonous. You can identify these by their lack of odor.

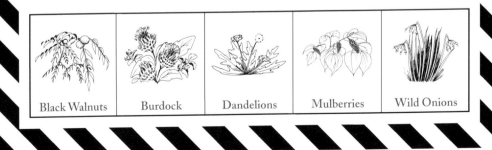

| Black Walnuts | Burdock | Dandelions | Mulberries | Wild Onions |

NOVEMBER

Monday **17**	Tuesday **18**	Wednesday **19**
		1620—The *Mayflower* reaches Cape Cod.

Thursday **20**	Friday **21**	Saturday **22**

		Sunday *New Moon* ● **23**
1497—Vasco da Gama rounds Cape of Good Hope, discovering a water route from Europe to India.		1945—The U.S. rationing of meat and butter during World War II comes to an end.

★ **Tip of the Week:**

Avoid touching or eating any plants you have not identified with 100 percent certainty. Some poisonous plants cause severe dermatitis (itching), while others can be handled safely but are poisonous if ingested.

November

S	M	T	W	T	F	S
						1
2	3	4	5	6	7	8
9	10	11	12	13	14	15
16	17	18	19	20	21	22
23/30	24	25	26	27	28	29

HOW TO SURVIVE IF YOU ARE IN THE LINE OF FIRE

1 Get as far away as possible.
An untrained shooter isn't likely to be accurate at any distance greater than sixty feet.

2 Run fast, but do not move in a straight line—weave back and forth to make it more difficult for the shooter to hit you.
The average shooter will not have the training necessary to hit a moving target at any real distance.

3 Turn a corner as quickly as you can, particularly if your pursuer has a rifle or assault weapon.
Rifles have much greater accuracy and range, and the person may be more likely to either aim or spray bullets in your direction.

4 Do not bother to count shots.
You will have no idea if the shooter has more ammunition. Counting is only for the movies.

Run in a zigzag pattern to make yourself more difficult to hit. (B)

(A)

Try to turn a corner if possible. (A)

(B)

NOVEMBER

Monday	Tuesday	Wednesday
24	**25**	**26**
1874—Barbed wire is patented by Joseph Glidden.	1867—Dynamite is patented by Alfred Nobel.	

Thursday	Friday	Saturday
27	**28**	**29**
		1929—American explorer Richard Byrd completes the first plane flight over the South Pole.

Sunday   *First Quarter* ☽

30

Thanksgiving

1989—The first U.S. liver transplant using a live donor is completed at the University of Chicago Medical Center.

1993—President Clinton signs the Brady handgun control bill into law, requiring a 5-day waiting period when purchasing a gun.

★ **Tip of the Week:**

If you are face to face with a shooter, do anything you can to make yourself less of a target. Turn sideways and stay low—stray bullets are likely to be at least a few feet above the ground. If the shooter is outside, stay inside and stay away from doors and windows.

November

S	M	T	W	T	F	S
						1
2	3	4	5	6	7	8
9	10	11	12	13	14	15
16	17	18	19	20	21	22
23/30	24	25	26	27	28	29

HOW TO SURVIVE
A MUGGING

1 Do not argue or fight with a mugger unless your life is clearly in danger.
If all a mugger wants is your purse, wallet, or other belongings, surrender them.
Your possessions are not worth your life.

2 If you are certain that your attacker means to do you or a loved one harm,
attack vital areas of your assailant's body.
Aim to disable your attacker with the first blow by:
- Thrusting your fingers into and above your attacker's eyes.
- Driving your knee in an upward direction into his groin (if the mugger
  is male).
- Striking the front of your attacker's throat, using the area between your
  thumb and first finger, or the side of your hand, held straight and strong.
- Slamming your elbow into the mugger's ribs.
- Stomping down on the mugger's instep.

3 Use an object as a weapon.
Many common objects can be effective weapons if they are aimed at vulnerable
body parts. Pick up and use what is easily available, whether it is a stick, your
keys, or a car antenna (all are good for slashing or jabbing at your attacker's face
and eyes).

DECEMBER

Monday **1**	Tuesday **2**	Wednesday **3**
		1967—The first heart transplant is performed.

Thursday **4**	Friday **5**	Saturday **6**
		Sunday **7**
1971—General Motors recalls over six million vehicles with possible motor mount failure.	1961—President Kennedy calls for broad participation by U.S. citizens in exercising regularly.	1869—First known bank robbery by the James Gang.

★ **Tip of the Week:**

To foil a pickpocket, carry a wallet that contains only a small amount of money and photo ID that is not your driver's license or passport. Use this wallet for daily small expenses. Wrap a rubber band around it so you will feel it if someone attempts to remove it.

December

S	M	T	W	T	F	S
	1	2	3	4	5	6
7	8	9	10	11	12	13
14	15	16	17	18	19	20
21	22	23	24	25	26	27
28	29	30	31			

HOW TO IDENTIFY
AND AVOID MINEFIELDS

There are four basic mine types:

TRIPWIRE MINES—Stepping across a wire attached to the detonator will cause the mine to explode.

DIRECT PRESSURE MINES—Stepping down on a pressure-sensitive pad will activate the detonator.

TIMER MINES—A timer can be an electrical clock, a digital clock, a dripping/mixing chemical, or a mechanical timer that will detonate the mine.

REMOTE MINES—A remote mine can be detonated via an electrical charge across a wire (a "clacker"), via a radio signal, or from a heat or sound sensor.

If you find yourself in a minefield, follow these steps to avoid detonating one.

1 Keep your eyes on your feet.

2 Do not move forward any further.

3 Look for spikes, detonators, wires, or bumps and discoloration in the ground around you.

4 Avoid these areas, and back up slowly in your own footsteps. Do not turn around. Walk backward.

5 Stop when you are certain you are safe.

DECEMBER

Monday *Full Moon* ○	Tuesday	Wednesday
8	**9**	**10**
		1996—The United Nations ratifies a U.S.-sponsored ban on mines.

Thursday	Friday	Saturday
11	**12**	**13**
		1577—Sir Francis Drake sets sail from England on a trip around the world.
		Sunday
		14
		1911—Norwegian explorer Roald Amundsen reaches the South Pole.

★ **Tip of the Week:**

When in a region where mines may be, such as a post-war country, look out for:

- Dirt that has been disturbed.
- Wires across trails.
- Newly destroyed vehicles on or just off the road.
- Brush, overgrown fields, and trails.
- Fields of dead animals.

December

S	M	T	W	T	F	S
	1	2	3	4	5	6
7	8	9	10	11	12	13
14	15	16	17	18	19	20
21	22	23	24	25	26	27
28	29	30	31			

HOW TO BUILD
A SNOW TRENCH

1 Map out a trench so that the opening is at a right angle to the prevailing wind. You need to find a space large enough so that the width and length are just a bit longer and taller than your body when lying down. You need only a minimal depth to maintain a cozy space for body heat conservation.

2 Dig the trench with a wider, flatter opening on one end for your head, using whatever tools you have or can create.
A cooking pan or long, flat piece of wood works well as an entrenching tool.

3 Cover the top of the trench with layers of branches, then a tarp, plastic sheeting, or whatever is available, then a thin layer of snow.
A "door" can be made using a backpack, blocks of snow, or whatever materials provide some ventilation and yet block the heat-robbing effects of the wind.

DECEMBER

Monday **15**	**Tuesday** *Last Quarter* ☽ **16**	**Wednesday** **17**

1903—The Wright brothers complete the first successful flight of a mechanically propelled airplane at Kitty Hawk, North Carolina.

1773—The Boston Tea Party takes place.

Thursday **18**	**Friday** **19**	**Saturday** **20** Chanukah

1868—Harvey Firestone, founder of Firestone Tire and Rubber Company, is born.

Sunday
21

1790—Arctic explorer Sir William Parry is born.

Winter Solstice

★ **Tip of the Week:**

If you cannot stay dry in the process of building a snow shelter, do not build it! Moving enough snow to create a shelter big enough for even just one person is hard work, and any contact of your skin or clothing with snow while digging will amplify your body's heat loss.

December

S	M	T	W	T	F	S
	1	2	3	4	5	6
7	8	9	10	11	12	13
14	15	16	17	18	19	20
21	22	23	24	25	26	27
28	29	30	31			

HOW TO TREAT FROSTBITE

1 Remove wet clothing and dress the area with warm, dry clothing.

2 Immerse frozen areas in warm water (100–105°F) or apply warm compresses for ten to thirty minutes.

3 If warm water is not available, wrap gently in warm blankets.

4 Avoid direct heat, including electric or gas fires, heating pads, and hot water bottles.

5 Never thaw the area if it is at risk of refreezing; this can cause severe tissue damage.

6 Do not rub frostbitten skin or rub snow on it, even if it needs cleaning.

7 Take a pain reliever such as aspirin or ibuprofen during rewarming to lessen the pain.
Rewarming will be accompanied by a severe burning sensation. There may be skin blistering and soft tissue swelling and the skin may turn red, blue, or purple in color. When skin is pink and no longer numb, the area is thawed.

8 Apply sterile dressings to the affected areas.
Place the dressing between fingers or toes if they have been affected. Try not to disturb any blisters, wrap rewarmed areas to prevent refreezing, and have the patient keep thawed areas as still as possible.

9 Get medical treatment as soon as possible.

After thawing the skin, sensation will return and it may be painful. Apply sterile dressings to the affected areas, placing it between toes or fingers if they have been frostbitten.

Severe frostbite may cause the skin to blister or swell. Wrap area to prevent refreezing, and seek medical treatment.

DECEMBER

Monday **22**	Tuesday *New Moon* ● **23**	Wednesday **24**
		1977—"Stayin' Alive" by the Bee Gees debuts on Billboard's Top 40.
Thursday **25**	Friday **26**	Saturday **27**
		Sunday **28**
Christmas	Kwanzaa Boxing Day (Canada)	

★ **Tip of the Week:**

To avoid frostbite and frostnip, keep extremities warm and covered in cold weather. Use layered clothing and a face mask. Wear mittens instead of gloves, and keep the ears covered. Take breaks from the cold to warm extremities whenever possible.

December

S	M	T	W	T	F	S
		1	2	3	4	5	6
7	8	9	10	11	12	13
14	15	16	17	18	19	20
21	22	23	24	25	26	27
28	29	30	31			

HOW TO CARRY SOMEONE WHO IS PASSED OUT

1 Prepare to lift by bending your knees and placing one arm under the person's back and the other under his or her knees.
Your arms should completely span the back so that your hand is on the person's side, and the backs of both knees should be on your other arm.

2 Lift the unconscious person by bending your knees, then standing up quickly, using the momentum to shift his or her body weight over your shoulder.
Use the strength of your legs and knees, holding them close to your body and keeping your back straight. Do not lift with your back. The person's torso should be hanging over your back, legs hanging over your front.

3 Walk to your destination.

4 Carefully put the person down by bending your knees and flopping them over onto a soft surface.
Keep your back straight.

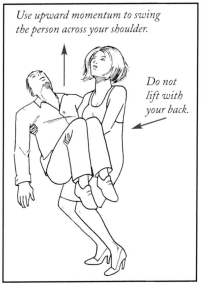

Use upward momentum to swing the person across your shoulder.

Do not lift with your back.

DECEMBER/JANUARY

Monday	Tuesday	*First Quarter* ☾	Wednesday
29	**30**		**31**
1800—Charles Goodyear, inventor of the rubber tire, is born.			1984—The nation's first mandatory seatbelt law goes into effect.

Thursday	Friday	Saturday
1	**2**	**3**

		Sunday
		4
New Year's Day		1885—The first successful appendectomy is performed.

★**Tip of the Week:**

Plan to carry the person for only a short distance—any further will become too difficult, increasing the risk of a fall, and you could both be injured.

December

S	M	T	W	T	F	S
		1	2	3	4	5	6
7	8	9	10	11	12	13
14	15	16	17	18	19	20
21	22	23	24	25	26	27
28	29	30	31			

January

S	M	T	W	T	F	S
					1	2	3
4	5	6	7	8	9	10
11	12	13	14	15	16	17
18	19	20	21	22	23	24
25	26	27	28	29	30	31

2002

January
S	M	T	W	T	F	S
		1	2	3	4	5
6	7	8	9	10	11	12
13	14	15	16	17	18	19
20	21	22	23	24	25	26
27	28	29	30	31		

February
S	M	T	W	T	F	S
					1	2
3	4	5	6	7	8	9
10	11	12	13	14	15	16
17	18	19	20	21	22	23
24	25	26	27	28		

March
S	M	T	W	T	F	S
					1	2
3	4	5	6	7	8	9
10	11	12	13	14	15	16
17	18	19	20	21	22	23
24/31	25	26	27	28	29	30

April
S	M	T	W	T	F	S
	1	2	3	4	5	6
7	8	9	10	11	12	13
14	15	16	17	18	19	20
21	22	23	24	25	26	27
28	29	30				

May
S	M	T	W	T	F	S
			1	2	3	4
5	6	7	8	9	10	11
12	13	14	15	16	17	18
19	20	21	22	23	24	25
26	27	28	29	30	31	

June
S	M	T	W	T	F	S
						1
2	3	4	5	6	7	8
9	10	11	12	13	14	15
16	17	18	19	20	21	22
23/30	24	25	26	27	28	29

July
S	M	T	W	T	F	S
	1	2	3	4	5	6
7	8	9	10	11	12	13
14	15	16	17	18	19	20
21	22	23	24	25	26	27
28	29	30	31			

August
S	M	T	W	T	F	S
				1	2	3
4	5	6	7	8	9	10
11	12	13	14	15	16	17
18	19	20	21	22	23	24
25	26	27	28	29	30	31

September
S	M	T	W	T	F	S
1	2	3	4	5	6	7
8	9	10	11	12	13	14
15	16	17	18	19	20	21
22	23	24	25	26	27	28
29	30					

October
S	M	T	W	T	F	S
		1	2	3	4	5
6	7	8	9	10	11	12
13	14	15	16	17	18	19
20	21	22	23	24	25	26
27	28	29	30	31		

November
S	M	T	W	T	F	S
					1	2
3	4	5	6	7	8	9
10	11	12	13	14	15	16
17	18	19	20	21	22	23
24	25	26	27	28	29	30

December
S	M	T	W	T	F	S
1	2	3	4	5	6	7
8	9	10	11	12	13	14
15	16	17	18	19	20	21
22	23	24	25	26	27	28
29	30	31				

2003

January
S	M	T	W	T	F	S
			1	2	3	4
5	6	7	8	9	10	11
12	13	14	15	16	17	18
19	20	21	22	23	24	25
26	27	28	29	30	31	

February
S	M	T	W	T	F	S
						1
2	3	4	5	6	7	8
9	10	11	12	13	14	15
16	17	18	19	20	21	22
23	24	25	26	27	28	

March
S	M	T	W	T	F	S
						1
2	3	4	5	6	7	8
9	10	11	12	13	14	15
16	17	18	19	20	21	22
$^{23}/_{30}$	$^{24}/_{31}$	25	26	27	28	29

April
S	M	T	W	T	F	S
		1	2	3	4	5
6	7	8	9	10	11	12
13	14	15	16	17	18	19
20	21	22	23	24	25	26
27	28	29	30			

May
S	M	T	W	T	F	S
				1	2	3
4	5	6	7	8	9	10
11	12	13	14	15	16	17
18	19	20	21	22	23	24
25	26	27	28	29	30	31

June
S	M	T	W	T	F	S
1	2	3	4	5	6	7
8	9	10	11	12	13	14
15	16	17	18	19	20	21
22	23	24	25	26	27	28
29	30					

July
S	M	T	W	T	F	S
		1	2	3	4	5
6	7	8	9	10	11	12
13	14	15	16	17	18	19
20	21	22	23	24	25	26
27	28	29	30	31		

August
S	M	T	W	T	F	S
					1	2
3	4	5	6	7	8	9
10	11	12	13	14	15	16
17	18	19	20	21	22	23
$^{24}/_{31}$	25	26	27	28	29	30

September
S	M	T	W	T	F	S
	1	2	3	4	5	6
7	8	9	10	11	12	13
14	15	16	17	18	19	20
21	22	23	24	25	26	27
28	29	30				

October
S	M	T	W	T	F	S
			1	2	3	4
5	6	7	8	9	10	11
12	13	14	15	16	17	18
19	20	21	22	23	24	25
26	27	28	29	30	31	

November
S	M	T	W	T	F	S
						1
2	3	4	5	6	7	8
9	10	11	12	13	14	15
16	17	18	19	20	21	22
$^{23}/_{30}$	24	25	26	27	28	29

December
S	M	T	W	T	F	S
	1	2	3	4	5	6
7	8	9	10	11	12	13
14	15	16	17	18	19	20
21	22	23	24	25	26	27
28	29	30	31			

2004

January

S	M	T	W	T	F	S
				1	2	3
4	5	6	7	8	9	10
11	12	13	14	15	16	17
18	19	20	21	22	23	24
25	26	27	28	29	30	31

February

S	M	T	W	T	F	S
1	2	3	4	5	6	7
8	9	10	11	12	13	14
15	16	17	18	19	20	21
22	23	24	25	26	27	28
29						

March

S	M	T	W	T	F	S
	1	2	3	4	5	6
7	8	9	10	11	12	13
14	15	16	17	18	19	20
21	22	23	24	25	26	27
28	29	30	31			

April

S	M	T	W	T	F	S
				1	2	3
4	5	6	7	8	9	10
11	12	13	14	15	16	17
18	19	20	21	22	23	24
25	26	27	28	29	30	

May

S	M	T	W	T	F	S
						1
2	3	4	5	6	7	8
9	10	11	12	13	14	15
16	17	18	19	20	21	22
23/30	24/31	25	26	27	28	29

June

S	M	T	W	T	F	S
		1	2	3	4	5
6	7	8	9	10	11	12
13	14	15	16	17	18	19
20	21	22	23	24	25	26
27	28	29	30			

July

S	M	T	W	T	F	S
				1	2	3
4	5	6	7	8	9	10
11	12	13	14	15	16	17
18	19	20	21	22	23	24
25	26	27	28	29	30	31

August

S	M	T	W	T	F	S
1	2	3	4	5	6	7
8	9	10	11	12	13	14
15	16	17	18	19	20	21
22	23	24	25	26	27	28
29	30	31				

September

S	M	T	W	T	F	S
			1	2	3	4
5	6	7	8	9	10	11
12	13	14	15	16	17	18
19	20	21	22	23	24	25
26	27	28	29	30		

October

S	M	T	W	T	F	S
					1	2
3	4	5	6	7	8	9
10	11	12	13	14	15	16
17	18	19	20	21	22	23
24/31	25	26	27	28	29	30

November

S	M	T	W	T	F	S
	1	2	3	4	5	6
7	8	9	10	11	12	13
14	15	16	17	18	19	20
21	22	23	24	25	26	27
28	29	30				

December

S	M	T	W	T	F	S
			1	2	3	4
5	6	7	8	9	10	11
12	13	14	15	16	17	18
19	20	21	22	23	24	25
26	27	28	29	30	31	

SURVIVAL NOTES

SURVIVAL NOTES

ABOUT THE EXPERTS

How to Jump from a Moving Car
Sources: Dale Gibson, stuntman, teacher of swordfighting skills to Hollywood actors and stunt people, sword fighting stuntman in *The Mask of Zorro*; Christopher Caso, stuntman, producer and performer of high-fall stunts for various movies, including *Batman and Robin*, *The Lost World*, and *The Crow: City of Angels*.

How to Survive a Hostage Situation
Source: The U.S. State Department.

How to Survive a Flash Flood
Source: Federal Emergency Management Administration Office of Meteorology; National Weather Service.

How to Survive Adrift at Sea
Source: Greta Schanen, managing editor of *Sailing* magazine.

How to Escape from a Mountain Lion
Sources: The National Park Service; The Texas Park and Wildlife Association; Chris Kallio, backpacking guide for About.com; Mary Taylor Gray, writer for *Colorado's Wildlife Company*, a publication of the Colorado Division of Wildlife.

How to Find Direction without a Compass
Sources: Jeff Randall and Mike Perrin, survival experts, owners of Randall's Adventure and Training (www.jungletraining.com), a service that guides extreme expeditions and facilitates training in the jungles of Central America and the Amazon basin of Peru; *U.S. Army Survival Manual*.

How to Survive in a Plummeting Elevator
Sources: Jay Preston, CSP, PE, general safety engineering consultant and forensic safety engineering specialist, former president of the Los Angeles Chapter of the American Society of Safety Engineers; Larry Holt, Senior Consultant at Elcon Elevator Controls and Consulting in Connecticut.

How to Stop a Car with Failed Brakes
Source: Vinny Minchillo, demolition derby driver, writer for a variety of automobile magazines including *AutoWeek*, *SportsCar*, and *Turbo*.

How to Treat a Scorpion Sting
Source: Scott Stockwell, U.S. Army major, combat medical entomologist, consultant on scorpion envenomation.

How to Survive an Avalanche
Source: Jim Frankenfield, director of the Cyberspace Snow and Avalanche Center, a nonprofit organization dedicated to avalanche safety education and information based in Oregon.

How to Survive When Lost in the Jungle
Sources: Jeff Randall and Mike Perrin.

How to Deal with a Stalker
Source: Julie Harman, Ph.D.

How to Fool a Lie Detector Test
Source: James F. Masucci, police officer for 17 years and detective for 12, owner of TCB Investigations & Consultant, a private investigation and security consulting business.

How to Get to the Surface if Your SCUBA Tank Runs Out of Air
Source: Graham Dickson, Professional Association of Diving Instructors (PADI) Master SCUBA instructor.

How to Make a Deadfall Animal Trap
Source: Ron Hood, survival expert, received wilderness training while a member of the U.S. Army and has taught wilderness survival classes for 20 years.

How to Break Down a Door
Source: David M. Lowell, certified master locksmith and education/proficiency registration program manager of the Associated Locksmiths of America, an industry trade group.

How to Stop a Runaway Horse
Sources: John and Kristy Milchick, horse trainers, owners and managers of Hideaway Stables in Kentucky.

How to Jump from a Moving Train
Source: Christopher Caso.

How to Climb out of a Well
Sources: Andrew P. Jenkins, Ph.D., WEMT, Professor of Community Health and Physical Education at Central Washington University; John Wehbring, mountaineering instructor, a member of the San Diego Mountain Rescue Team, former chairman of the Mountain Rescue Association (California region), and teacher of the Sierra Club's Basic Mountaineering course; Jon Lloyd, adventure consultant with VLM Adventure Consultants in the United Kingdom (www.vlmadventureconsultants.co.uk).

How to Avoid and Survive a Hit and Run
Source: Christopher Caso.

How to Escape from a Sinking Car
Sources: The U.S. Army's Cold Regions Research and Engineering Lab in New Hampshire; *Danger! Thin Ice*, a publication of the Minnesota Department of Natural Resources; Tim Smalley, Boating and Water Safety Education Coordinator for the Minnesota Department of Natural Resources.

How to Jump from Roof to Roof
Source: Christopher Caso.

How to Save Someone Who Is Choking
Source: Dr. James Li, Division of Emergency Medicine at Harvard Medical School in Cambridge, Massachusetts, instructor for the American College of Surgeons' course for physicians, Advanced Trauma Life Support.

How to Cross a Piranha-Infested River
Sources: Paul Cripps, Director of Amazonas Explorer, an organization specializing in adventure travel in Peru and Bolivia; Dr. David Schleser, researcher and eco-travel guide, author of *Piranhas: Everything About Selection, Care, Nutrition, Diseases, Breeding, and Behavior (More Complete Pet Owner's Manuals)*; Barry Tedder, marine biologist and jungle survival expert; Dr Peter Henderson, director of Pisces Conservation Ltd. Lymington, England (www.irchouse.demon.co.uk).

How to Avoid Being Struck by Lightning
Source: John Linder, director of the Wilderness Survival School for the Denver division of the Colorado Mountain Club, manager of the Snow Operations Training Center, an organization that teaches mountain survival skills to power companies and search and rescue teams.

Essential Survival Knowledge: How to Survive a Wild Animal Bite
Sources: The Erie County (PA) Department of Health, The National Institute of Allergy and Infectious Diseases, a division of the National Institute of Health; *The Columbia University College of Physicians and Surgeons Complete Home Medical Guide*.

How to Survive a Riot in a Foreign Country
Source: The Chief Consultant (who must remain anonymous) of Real World Rescue, a small, high-risk travel security company based in San Diego, California, that trains elite U.S. Government Special Operations personnel and Federal law enforcement agents on international terrorism and Third World survival (www.realworldrescue.com).

How to Survive a Nuclear Explosion
Source: *The U.S. Army Survival Manual*.

How to Survive a Sandstorm
Sources: Thomas E. Gill, Adjunct Professor in the Department of Geosciences and a Research Associate at the Wind Engineering Research Center of Texas Tech University and Jeffrey A. Lee, Associate Professor in the Department of Economics and Geography at Texas Tech, members of the Texas Wind Erosion Research PersonS (TWERPS), an informal research group of scientists and engineers from the U.S. Department of Agriculture and Texas Tech who study blowing sand and dust storms; The Office of Meteorology, National Weather Service; The U.S. Army Medical Research & Material Command.

How to Survive in Frigid Water
Source: Tim Smalley.

How to Perform a Tracheotomy
Source: Dr. Jeff Heit, director of internal medicine at a Philadelphia area hospital.

How to Survive a Tsunami
Sources: Eddie Bernard, Ph.D., director of the Pacific Marine Environmental Laboratory, leader of the U.S. team in the 1993 Sea of Japan tsunami damage survey, and director of the Pacific Tsunami Warning Center; the National Tsunami Hazard Mitigation Program; the NOAA Tsunami Research Program; the International Tsunami Information Center.

How to Survive When Lost in the Mountains
Source: John Linder.

How to Escape from Quicksand
Source: Karl S. Kruszelnicki, Julius Summer Miller Fellow at the School of Physics of the University of Sydney, Australia, author of several books on physics and natural phenomena, including *Flying Lasers, Robofish, Cities of Slime, and Other Brain-Bending Science Moments.*

How to Catch Fish without a Rod
Sources: Jean-Philippe Soule, leader of the Central American Sea Kayak Expedition 2000, former member of the elite French Mountain Commando unit; *The U.S. Army Survival Manual.*

How to Survive if You Are Attacked by Leeches
Source: Mark E. Siddall, Assistant Curator for the Division of Invertebrate Zoology at the American Museum of Natural History in New York City.

How to Survive a Riptide
Sources: The National Weather Service in Miami, Florida; Dr. Robert Budman ("The Surf Doctor"), American Board of Family Practice certified physician and *Surfer* magazine's medical advisor; the Californial Surf Life Saving Association.

How to Use a Defibrillator to Restore a Heartbeat
Sources: Dr. Jeff Heit; Tom Costello, district manager of Hewlett-Packard; Heartstream; The American Heart Association.

How to Ram Your Car Through a Barricade
Source: Vinny Minchillo.

How to Escape from the Trunk of a Car
Source: Janette E. Fennell, founder of TRUNC (Trunk Releases Urgently Needed Coalition; www.netkitchen.com/trunc), a non-profit whose mission is to make sure children and adults trapped in trunks can escape safely.

How to Survive if Your Parachute Fails to Open
Source: Joe Jennings, skydiving cinematographer and skydiving coordination specialist, designed, coordinated, and filmed skydiving stunts for numerous television commercials, including Mountain Dew, Pepsi, MTV Sports, Coca-Cola, and ESPN.

How to Survive a Fall onto Subway Tracks
Source: Joseph Brennan, author of *The Guide to Abandoned Subway Stations (Disused or Unused Underground Railway Stations of the New York Area)*.

How to Escape a Bad Date
Source: Antonio J. Mendez, retired CIA intelligence officer, author of *The Master of Disguise: My Secret Life in the CIA*.

Essential Survival Knowledge: Plants You Can Eat
Source: "Wildman" Steve Brill, naturalist, author of *Identifying and Harvesting Edible and Medicinal Plants in Wild (and Not-So-Wild) Places; The U.S. Army Survival Manual*.

How to Survive if You Are in the Line of Fire
Source: Brady Geril, vice president of Product Management for the Counter Spy Shops, the retail division of CCS International Ltd. of London.

How to Survive a Mugging
Source: George Arrington, self-defense instructor, teacher of self-defense for more than 25 years, 4th-degree Black Belt, licensed instructor of Danzan-Ryu Jujutsu.

How to Identify and Avoid Minefields
Sources: Jeff Randall and Mike Perrin.

How to Build a Snow Trench
Source: John Linder.

How to Treat Frostbite
Source: John Linder.

How to Carry Someone Who Is Passed Out
Source: Vince Christopher, physical therapist and amateur weightlifter in New York, New York.

About the Authors

Joshua Piven, a computer journalist and freelance writer, has been chased by knife-wielding motorcycle bandits, stuck in subway tunnels, robbed and mugged, has had to break down doors and pick locks, and crashes his computer regularly. He is the co-author of *The Worst-Case Scenario Survival Handbook* series and lives in Philadelphia with his wife.

David Borgenicht is the president of Quirk Books and the author of *The Worst-Case Scenario Survival Handbook* series with Joshua Piven, as well as *The Jewish Mother Goose* (Running Press, 2000), and *The Little Book of Stupid Questions* (Hysteria, 1999). He has ridden in heavily armored vehicles in Pakistan, stowed away on Amtrak, and broken into several houses (each for good reason). He, too, lives in Philadelphia with his wife.

Brenda Brown is a freelance illustrator and cartoonist whose work has appeared in many books and major publications, including *The Worst-Case Scenario Survival Handbook* series, *Reader's Digest*, *The Saturday Evening Post*, *The National Enquirer*, and *Federal Lawyer and National Review*. Her digital graphics have been incorporated into software programs developed by Adobe Systems, Deneba Software, Corel Corp., and many Web sites.

Check out www.worstcasescenarios.com for new scenarios, updates, and more!